European Computer Driving Licence®

ECDL Advanced

Syllabus 2.0

Module AM4 - Spreadsheets

Using Microsoft® Excel 2003

Release ECDL227v1

Published by:

> CiA Training Ltd
> Business & Innovation Centre
> Sunderland Enterprise Park
> Sunderland SR5 2TH
> United Kingdom
>
> Tel: +44 (0) 191 549 5002
> Fax: +44 (0) 191 549 9005
>
> E-mail: info@ciatraining.co.uk
> Web: www.ciatraining.co.uk
>
> **ISBN-13: 978 1 86005 652 9**

This training, which has been approved by ECDL Foundation, includes exercise items intended to assist Candidates in their training for an ECDL Certification Programme. These exercises are not ECDL Foundation certification tests. For information about authorised Test Centres in different national territories, please refer to the ECDL Foundation website at www.ecdl.org

First published 2009

European Computer Driving Licence, ECDL, International Computer Driving Licence, ICDL, e-Citizen and related logos are all registered Trade Marks of The European Computer Driving Licence Foundation Limited ("ECDL Foundation").

CiA Training Ltd is an entity independent of ECDL Foundation and is not associated with ECDL Foundation in any manner. This courseware may be used to assist candidates to prepare for the ECDL Foundation Certification Programme as titled on the courseware. Neither ECDL Foundation nor **CiA Training Ltd** warrants that the use of this courseware publication will ensure passing of the tests for that ECDL Foundation Certification Programme. This courseware publication has been independently reviewed and approved by ECDL Foundation as covering the learning objectives for the ECDL Foundation Certification Programme.

Confirmation of this approval can be obtained by reviewing the Partners Page in the About Us Section of the website www.ecdl.org

The material contained in this courseware publication has not been reviewed for technical accuracy and does not guarantee that candidates will pass the test for the ECDL Foundation Certification Programme. Any and all assessment items and/or performance-based exercises contained in this courseware relate solely to this publication and do not constitute or imply certification by ECDL Foundation in respect of the ECDL Foundation Certification Programme or any other ECDL Foundation test. Irrespective of how the material contained in this courseware is deployed, for example in a learning management system (LMS) or a customised interface, nothing should suggest to the candidate that this material constitutes certification or can lead to certification through any other process than official ECDL Foundation certification testing.

For details on sitting a test for an ECDL Foundation certification programme, please contact your country's designated National Licensee or visit the ECDL Foundation's website at www.ecdl.org.

Candidates using this courseware must be registered with the National Operator before undertaking a test for an ECDL Foundation Certification Programme. Without a valid registration, the test(s) cannot be undertaken and no certificate, nor any other form of recognition, can be given to a candidate. Registration should be undertaken with your country's designated National Licensee at an Approved Test Centre.

Downloading the Data Files

The data associated with these exercises must be downloaded from our website. Go to: *www.ciatraining.co.uk/data*. Follow the on screen instructions to download the appropriate data files.

By default, the data files will be downloaded to **My Documents\CIA DATA FILES\Advanced ECDL\AM4 Excel 2003 Data**.

If you prefer, the data can be supplied on CD at an additional cost. Contact the Sales team at *info@ciatraining.co.uk*.

Aims

To provide the student with an understanding of the more advanced spreadsheet concepts of spreadsheet models using *Excel*.

Objectives

After completing the guide the user will be able to:

- Create and maintain complex spreadsheets
- Manipulate charts
- Create and use Scenarios
- Create and use Templates
- Link cells, worksheets and workbooks
- Use complicated Functions of various types
- Use Data Tables and Databases
- Create and use simple Macros
- Use Auditing techniques to check for errors

Assessment of Knowledge

At the end of this guide is a section called the **Record of Achievement Matrix**. Before the guide is started it is recommended that the user complete the matrix to measure the level of current knowledge.

Tick boxes are provided for each feature. **1** is for no knowledge, **2** some knowledge and **3** is for competent.

After working through a section, complete the **Record of Achievement Matrix** for that section and only when competent in all areas move on to the next section.

Contents

Section 1
Introduction

By the end of this Section you should be able to:

Understand Spreadsheet Design

Identify the Different Techniques to Use

To gain an understanding of the above features, work through the **Driving Lessons** in this **Section**.

For each **Driving Lesson**, read the **Park and Read** instructions, without touching the keyboard, then work through the numbered steps of the **Manoeuvres** on the computer. Complete the **Revision Exercise(s)** at the end of the section to test your knowledge.

Driving Lesson 1 - Spreadsheet Design

P Park and Read

Whilst any course on advanced spreadsheet applications needs to describe and explain the techniques necessary to produce successful worksheets, thought should always be given to the overall purpose of the finished spreadsheet and to the intended users.

Structure

Excel supports multi-sheet workbooks. A saved spreadsheet file is called a workbook. Each workbook can contain a vast number of worksheets. Each worksheet is a spreadsheet. Information can be passed from sheet to sheet, enabling large complicated models to be created using simpler smaller parts. For a company this is invaluable, different members of staff can provide data that feeds into "a bigger picture" worksheet, one where all the totals can be collected without the minute detail.

Purpose

Every worksheet produced has a purpose. Before starting to create a worksheet, take some time to consider the purpose behind it, how it will be used and the results that it needs to present, then plan the design accordingly.

Example 1. You are creating a spreadsheet to input and display departmental budgets and consolidate them into an overall company budget. Will each department complete its own piece of the worksheet, or will it be more efficient to have separate worksheets for each department and join them together later as a separate process? Will the results need to be incorporated into a larger financial report, in which case the formatting and structure will need to be compatible?

Example 2. You are creating a spreadsheet to record membership details for a club or gym. You need to know what the list will be used for. Does it need to record payment of fees? Will it be used to analyse membership over various activities or groups? If so, relevant details need to be included. Will it be used to send out letters to members? If so, it will need to include names and addresses.

Example 3. You are creating a spreadsheet to present statistical viewing figures for a television channel. Does it need to show a series of charts without the original data, or just the data so that users can create their own charts? What analysis will be required? If it needs to be analysed by region for example, then regional information must be included with the original data.

Driving Lesson 1 - Continued

Audience

The intended users of your spreadsheet have a major impact on the way it is designed in two areas.

Firstly, in the way it is presented. A company financial report for the Financial Director may need to have summary information analysed by various factors, using pivot tables and charts for example. The same data for an accountant or auditor may need to see the detailed breakdown of all totals into the individual items that make them up.

Secondly, many practical spreadsheets are dynamic, i.e. they will require frequent updating, and so users will be using your spreadsheet for data input and manipulation. Are your users going to merely read the data you give them, or are they expecting to analyse it themselves using filters and sorts, for example? Make sure your design takes into account the competence of the people who will be doing this.

Other Considerations

There are often practical considerations to spreadsheet design. A working spreadsheet can in principle be as large as you like, but scrolling horizontally and vertically in a spreadsheet can become confusing. Try to arrange the layout so that scrolling is only necessary in one direction, or it may be better to split the solution into several linked worksheets where possible.

The final form of your spreadsheet may also affect its style. You may be asked to produce a spreadsheet that will be used on a web page or presentation slide. This will require that the final result is compact enough for this purpose.

Driving Lesson 2 - Techniques to Use

▣ Park and Read

Spreadsheet software such as *Microsoft Excel* enables you to produce professional looking, functional worksheets for many different purposes. No matter what type of job you do, it's likely that at some stage you will need a list or table of data that requires some kind of manipulation or numerical processing, e.g. sorting, filtering or totalling and a spreadsheet would be the best solution for such a task.

In particular, *Excel* has many features that allow you to create complex spreadsheets, i.e. multi page sheets containing a variety of formatting styles and techniques and possibly containing various analysis and graphical presentations. Some of the relevant skills and techniques are:

- **Advanced editing and formatting**. Including custom and conditional formatting, hiding selected data and using subtotalling.

- **Templates**. Allowing many worksheets to be based on the same consistent style.

- **Security**. Restricting access to spreadsheets or protecting the content of certain cells within spreadsheets from accidental editing.

- **Linking**. Links to data within worksheets, between worksheets and between different workbooks.

- **Lists**. The specific features which can be used when the spreadsheet is in a list format.

- **Sorting**. Including custom sorts.

- **Querying/Filtering**. Including advanced filtering options.

- **Charts and Graphs**. Including formatting and modifying of various chart types.

- **Functions**. Using a wide range of functions, including numerical, text, logical and lookup. Also includes complex formulas with nested functions.

- **Analysis techniques**. Including pivot tables, scenarios, and data tables.

- **Auditing**. Including error tracing, formula display and working with comments.

- **Macros**. Instructions to perform repetitive tasks with a single command.

- **Links**. To allow users of the documentation to access relevant data from other sources.

Driving Lesson 3 - Revision: Introduction

This is not an ECDL test. Testing may only be carried out through certified ECDL test centres. This covers the features introduced in this section. Try not to refer to the preceding Driving Lessons while completing it.

1. When designing a spreadsheet, what are the advantages of splitting a large task into several smaller tasks using different worksheets/workbooks?

2. When designing a large spreadsheet why should it either fit horizontally or vertically on the screen, if possible?

3. When creating a spreadsheet for others why is protection of the data so important?

4. After creating a spreadsheet for others to use, what other tasks may you be required to do?

5. If you were a designer and seller of kitchens or bathrooms, what techniques might you use when creating supporting spreadsheets?

6. What is a template?

7. What is a macro?

8. If you were charged with assembling the sales figures for a company, how would you present them?

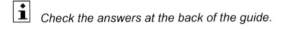 *Check the answers at the back of the guide.*

If you experienced any difficulty completing this Revision refer back to the Driving Lessons in this section. Then redo the Revision.

Once you are confident with the features, complete the Record of Achievement Matrix referring to the section at the end of the guide. Only when competent move on to the next Section.

Section 2
Formatting

By the end of this Section you should be able to:

Split Windows

Use Conditional Formatting

Use AutoFormat

Use Paste Special

Transpose Data

Copy and Move Sheets

To gain an understanding of the above features, work through the **Driving Lessons** in this **Section**.

For each **Driving Lesson**, read the **Park and Read** instructions, without touching the keyboard, then work through the numbered steps of the **Manoeuvres** on the computer. Complete the **Revision Exercise(s)** at the end of the section to test your knowledge.

Driving Lesson 4 - Split a Window

Park and Read

Split is similar to freeze panes except that the individual panes can be scrolled to show different information in each pane.

Manoeuvres

1. Open the workbook **Retail** (see page 4 - **Downloading the Data Files** for the location).

2. **Split** is created at the active cell position. Click on cell **F8**.

3. Select **Window | Split**. The worksheet is now split into four areas, all displaying the same worksheet.

4. Move the active cell to the right and up a few cells, using the arrow keys.

5. Try clicking on each of the four scroll bars. Different parts of the worksheet move around, creating four different views of the same worksheet - very useful if using a large worksheet.

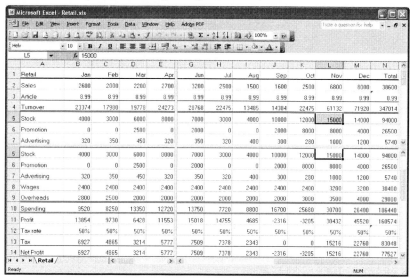

6. The split can be moved by clicking on the split lines and dragging them when ⁺‖⁺ appears. Drag the vertical split to the left to display only 2 columns in the left panes.

7. To remove the **Split** select **Window | Remove Split**.

8. Leave the workbook **Retail** open for the next Driving Lesson.

Driving Lesson 5 - Conditional Formatting

Park and Read

As well as applying formatting to certain cells, it is possible to apply different formatting to cells depending on the values within those cells. Selected cells can be compared to a value, or the results of a formula, to decide which format should be used. This is called **Conditional Formatting**.

Multiple conditions can be used to determine the formatting for the same cell, so for example, a cell could be coloured red if it is below a certain value and blue if it is greater than another value.

Manoeuvres

1. The workbook **Retail** should be open, if not, open it.

2. Highlight the **Turnover** figures, the range **B4:M4**.

3. Select **Format | Conditional Formatting**. The **Conditional Formatting** dialog box is displayed.

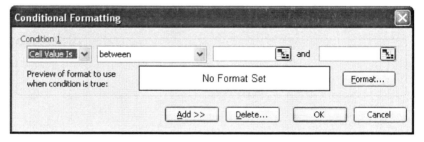

4. In the drop down criteria box (**between**) select **less than or equal to**. Enter the value **19000** in the next box.

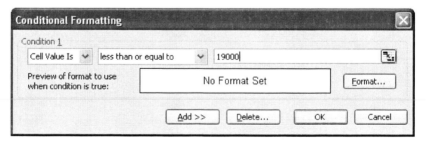

i *If entering a formula in the value box remember to start with =*

5. Click the **Format** button and select the font colour **Red**. Click **OK**.

Driving Lesson 5 - Continued

6.　To add another condition, click **Add**, select **greater than** and enter **25000** in the next box. Format the text to be **bold** and **blue**. Click **OK** and **OK** again to apply the formatting.

7.　Highlight the range **B14:M14** and apply the conditional formatting, values **less than** the average of the range **=Average($B$14:$M$14)** with a **pale yellow** cell shading. Click **OK** and **OK** again.

8.　To remove the **Conditional Formatting**, highlight the range **B4:M4** and select **Format | Conditional Formatting**. Click **Delete**.

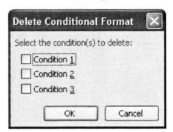

9.　Check **Condition 2**. Click **OK** and **OK** again. All values of over **25000** should now not be **blue** or **bold**.

10.　Experiment with adding and removing conditional formats to highlight results in a way that had not been possible before.

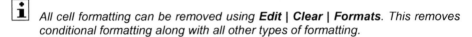

*All cell formatting can be removed using **Edit | Clear | Formats**. This removes conditional formatting along with all other types of formatting.*

11.　Close the workbook <u>without</u> saving.

Driving Lesson 6 - AutoFormat

▣ Park and Read

There is a set of pre-defined worksheet formats to enhance the appearance of a worksheet, via the **AutoFormat** command.

↱ Manoeuvres

1. Open the workbook **Budget**.

2. Highlight the range **A1:N14** and select **Format | AutoFormat**.

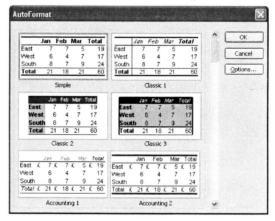

3. There is a list of the available **Table Formats** in the form of a **Sample**. Scroll through the list of **Table Formats**, to view each of the available options. Select **Accounting 2** and then click **OK**.

4. The sheet is now formatted in the **Accounting 2** style. Notice that some of the numbers have been incorrectly formatted as currency. Look at the **Sales** and **Tax rate** rows. This can be a problem when using **AutoFormat**.

5. To remove the format, select the range **A1:N14** and select **Edit | Clear | Formats**.

6. Select the range **A1:N14** and select **Format | AutoFormat**. From the list, select **Accounting 3** and click on the **Options** button.

7. There is now a choice of which parts of the format to apply to the selected range. Uncheck **Number** so that the number format is not applied. Note that the sample also changes as the options are changed.

ⓘ *Options within **AutoFormat** cannot be changed once they have been applied. Clear the **AutoFormat** and reapply with the selected options.*

8. Click on **OK** to apply the format to the worksheet. Try applying the other **AutoFormats** to the sheet. Close the workbook <u>without</u> saving.

Driving Lesson 7 - Paste Special

P Park and Read

When using **Copy** and **Paste** or **Cut** and **Paste**, the default is to paste the cell exactly as it was originally. **Paste Special** is used to paste cell information when a complete copy is not required. For example, **Paste Special** can:

- Paste only formulas, values or formats. Pasting values from cells that contain formulas is a way of fixing the data, as it will never then be recalculated.

- Combine ranges using an operation, e.g. adding, subtracting, etc.

- Transpose ranges (change a spreadsheet round by converting rows to columns and columns to rows).

- Paste links to the original data (covered in a later section).

Manoeuvres

1. Open the workbook **Finances** then open the workbook **Outgoings**.

2. In the workbook **Outgoings**, select the range **A1:L10** and click on the **Copy** button.

3. Click on the icon representing the **Finances** workbook on the **Taskbar** to make it active.

4. Click on cell **B5**. Select **Edit | Paste** or the **Paste** button to paste the contents normally.

i *To avoid confusion, the data can be pasted to an empty area of the sheet and then moved.*

5. Data can be pasted using a mathematical operation. Open the file **Income** and highlight the range **A1:L2**, the income figures.

6. Click the **Copy** button.

7. Switch back to **Finances** using either the **Window** command or the **Taskbar**.

8. The income figures are to go into the range **B2:M3** but this range already contains data, which would be overwritten if a normal paste was used. To keep the original data, select cell **B2** then select **Edit | Paste Special**.

Driving Lesson 7 - Continued

9. Under **Operation** click **Add** to add the two sets of figures together, then click **OK**. The data is now combined.

i *The **Add** operation was used in this example. **Subtract**, **Multiply** and **Divide** work in the same way.*

10. It may be required to convert formulas to values because the numbers are final, e.g. a VAT return or expenditure after the month end, etc. Using the **Finances** workbook, January has ended and the figures in column B are required to be converted to values. Check the cells **B4**, **B15** and **B16** to see that they contain formulas.

11. Select the range **B2:B16**.

12. Click **Copy**.

13. Select **Edit | Paste Special**.

14. Under **Paste**, select the **Values** option and click **OK**. Press **<Esc>** to remove the selection.

15. Check that the cells **B4**, **B15** and **B16** contain values.

i *Remember that this process removes formulas and therefore the worksheet cannot be used again. If repeated use is required, create and use a template.*

16. Save the workbook as **Finances2** and close it.

17. Close the workbooks **Income** and **Outgoings** <u>without</u> saving.

Driving Lesson 8 - Transposing Data

▣ Park and Read

It is sometimes necessary to change the way data is stored in a worksheet. Data stored in rows may be needed in columns and vice versa. This process is called **Transposing Data**.

⮑ Manoeuvres

1. Open the workbook **Transpose**. The **Result** column is needed in a row.

2. Select the range **B3:C17**, then select **Copy**.

3. Move to **A20** and select **Edit | Paste Special**. Check the **Transpose** box.

4. Click **OK**. Press **<Esc>** to exit the copy command.

5. The data is now shown in rows. Notice that the formats, i.e. the borders, have also been copied. This could have been avoided by selecting to paste just **Values** in the **Paste Special** dialog box.

6. Transpose the range **B3:C17**, with values only, to **A23**.

7. Close the workbook <u>without</u> saving.

8. Open the workbook **Budget**.

9. Transpose the range **A1:N14** to cell **A18**. Highlight the new range and remove all the borders. Add new borders as appropriate.

10. Check the formulas and print a landscape copy of the worksheet on one page.

11. Close the workbook <u>without</u> saving.

Driving Lesson 9 - Copying and Moving Sheets

▣ Park and Read

Sheets within a workbook can be moved or copied within the same workbook or to a different workbook.

↱ Manoeuvres

1. Open the workbook **Divisions**.

2. Sheets can be moved and copied within the same workbook by dragging the sheet tab with the mouse. Move the **North Midlands** sheet to between **South Wales** and **Midlands** by clicking and dragging the tab to the correct position (the black triangle always shows where the sheet will be inserted).

🛈 *Use the **Sheet navigation** buttons to locate the sheets that are not visible.*

3. Move the **North West** sheet to between **North** and **North East**.

4. A sheet is copied within the same workbook by holding <**Ctrl**> while dragging the sheet tab. To make a copy of the **North** sheet, hold down <**Ctrl**> and click and drag the **North** sheet tab across to the right, next to **North**. Release the mouse button first before <**Ctrl**>.

🛈 *The name of the copied sheet is **North (2)**. Duplicate sheet names are not allowed.*

5. If a sheet is to be moved or copied to another workbook the shortcut menu is used. Right click on the **North (2)** sheet tab.

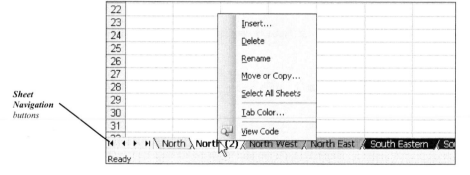

6. This menu controls all the actions relating to sheets. Select **Move or Copy**.

Exercise 9 - Continued

7. To create a copy the **Create a copy** box is checked, otherwise the sheet is moved. Check the **Create a copy** box.

8. To move or copy to a different workbook, select from the **To book** box. Drop down the list and select **(new book)**.

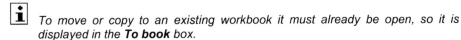 *To move or copy to an existing workbook it must already be open, so it is displayed in the **To book** box.*

9. The **Before sheet** box is empty for a new workbook. An existing one would display all the sheets for a selection to be made on the placement. Click **OK**.

10. A new workbook is started with just the sheet **North (2)** in it. Click **Divisions** on the **Taskbar** and check that **North (2)** is still in this book and that it was copied.

11. Close both workbooks <u>without</u> saving.

Driving Lesson 10 - Revision: Formatting

This is not an ECDL test. Testing may only be carried out through certified ECDL test centres. This covers the features introduced in this section. Try not to refer to the preceding Driving Lessons while completing it.

1. Open the workbook **House**.

2. Format the range **B2:N16** as currency with two decimal places.

3. Freeze the column and row titles.

4. Scroll off the screen to check that the titles are frozen.

5. Use **AutoFormat** to format the whole worksheet in **Classic 2** style.

6. The screen is cluttered, change the row height of rows **2** to **16** to **15.00** units.

7. The screen is still over cluttered with zeros, reformat the range **B2:N16** as **Currency** with no decimal places, to remove some of them.

8. Apply conditional formatting to the range **B16:N16** the accumulated savings row, to display amounts greater than **1000** to be bold and displayed in blue text and saving levels under **0** in bold and displayed in red text.

9. An unexpected windfall comes in the form of a **£500** pay bonus in **February**. Make the necessary change. Note the effects of the conditional formatting on row **16**.

10. Highlight the range **A1:N16** and using paste special make a copy on **Sheet2** but paste only the values.

11. Check the cells in rows **4**, **15** and **16** that contained formulas but are now just numbers. Change cell **B2** to **0**. It has no impact on any other cells.

12. Save the workbook as **House2**.

13. Close the workbook.

If you experienced any difficulty completing this Revision refer back to the Driving Lessons in this section. Then redo the Revision.

Once you are confident with the features, complete the Record of Achievement Matrix referring to the section at the end of the guide. Only when competent move on to the next Section.

Section 3
Protection

By the end of this Section you should be able to:

Protect Cells

Hide and Unhide Columns and Rows

Create Read-Only Workbooks

Hide and Unhide Worksheets & Workbooks

Protect Workbooks

Hide Formulas

To gain an understanding of the above features, work through the **Driving Lessons** in this **Section**.

For each **Driving Lesson**, read the **Park and Read** instructions, without touching the keyboard, then work through the numbered steps of the **Manoeuvres** on the computer. Complete the **Revision Exercise(s)** at the end of the section to test your knowledge.

Driving Lesson 11 - Protection

▣ Park and Read

Varying levels of protection can be applied to workbooks, individual worksheets and cells within worksheets. Opening sensitive files or data can be controlled by using passwords, either by preventing access completely or allowing files to be examined but not amended (Read Only access).

Specific areas within spreadsheets can be protected from accidental or deliberate alteration, by applying cell locking.

The following protection is available:

Passwords   prevent the workbooks from being opened by unauthorised users.

Cell Locking   prevents important cell data (usually formulas) from being amended or deleted. Cell locking is only activated when worksheet protection is switched on.

Workbooks   can have passwords added to them. They can be made **Read Only** to prevent changes.

Worksheets   can have cells locked to prevent changes and optionally, a password added to protect locked data and worksheet structure. A protected worksheet can only have data entered into unlocked cells and formatting cannot be carried out. When worksheet protection is disabled (the default) all cells are accessible whether locked or not.

Driving Lesson 12 - Worksheet & Cell Protection

P Park and Read

Worksheets can be protected with passwords so that no changes can be made to the locked cells within them.

By default all cells on a worksheet are locked, but this has no effect until worksheet protection is activated.

To allow changes to be made to some cells but not others when the worksheet is protected, it is necessary to unlock the editable cells, prior to adding the protection. This is often used when providing a spreadsheet for other users for data entry. All titles and formulas are locked to prevent changes, and only the cells where data is to be entered are unlocked and therefore accessible.

Manoeuvres

1. Open the workbook **Invoices**.

2. To protect the worksheet from changes, select **Tools | Protection | Protect Sheet**.

3. Entering a password is optional (be careful when using passwords as access to protected worksheets is prohibited without the password). Type **pass**. The password appears as ******** it is not displayed on the screen. Click **OK**.

i *Passwords are case sensitive.*

4. Confirm the password by typing **pass** again. Click **OK**.

5. Click on any cell and try to enter anything. No changes can be made to any cell on the worksheet. *Excel* displays the following message.

6. Click **OK** to remove the message.

Driving Lesson 12 - Continued

7. To remove the protection, select **Tools | Protection | Unprotect Sheet**, enter the password **pass** and click **OK** to remove the worksheet protection.

8. To allow changes to cells on a protected sheet, the required cells must first be **unlocked**. Select the range **E6:E14**. These are the cells that may be changed after protection has been added.

9. Select **Format | Cells** and choose the **Protection** tab. The protection of the range may now be set. The default is **Locked**, but not **Hidden**.

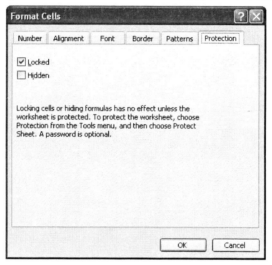

10. To unlock the cells in the selected range, click on **Locked** to uncheck it. Click **OK** (for access to more cells repeat the process for each range).

11. Having unlocked the required cells, to take effect, the worksheet has to be protected. Select **Tools | Protection | Protect Sheet**.

> *Remember that a password is optional and can be omitted, but the protection can then be removed by using the **Unprotect Sheet** command.*

12. Enter the password **pass** and click **OK**.

13. Confirm the password by typing **pass** again. Click **OK**.

14. Move to **E7** and change the contents to **£1500.00**.

15. Move to **F7** and try to change the **VAT** to **£250**. This cell is locked. Only the **Amount** column may be changed, i.e. the range **E6:E14**, that was unlocked. Click **OK**.

16. Change cell **E10** to **750**. This is allowed as the cell is unlocked.

17. Close the workbook **Invoices** <u>without</u> saving the changes.

Driving Lesson 13 - Hiding Rows & Columns

▣ Park and Read

Rows and/or **Columns** of sensitive data can be hidden from view. The data in any hidden rows and columns is still included in calculations, so that the results of the sheet are unaffected.

⌒ Manoeuvres

1.　Open the workbook **Budget**.

2.　Highlight the rows **5** and **6**. Select **Format | Row | Hide**. Rows 5 and 6 have now been hidden.

	A	B	C	D	E	F
1	Budget	Jan	Feb	Mar	Apr	May
2	Sales	6000	6400	7200	6200	5300
3	Price	6	6	6	6	6
4	Turnover	36000	38400	43200	37200	31800
7	Wages	6400	6400	6400	6400	6400
8	Materials	20800	22400	25600	21600	18000
9	Overheads	5000	5000	5000	5000	5000

Rows 5 and 6 are hidden. Note that row 7 still calculates Wages.

3.　To re-display rows **5** and **6**, highlight a range in row **4** to row **7**, e.g. **A4:A7** and select **Format | Row | Unhide**.

4.　A column can be hidden in a similar way, but another method is to use the shortcut menu. Right click on the column heading **F** and select **Hide**.

5.　To re-display column **F**, select columns **E** to **G**, right click and select **Unhide**.

6.　Columns and rows may also be hidden by dragging their borders until the column width or the row height is zero. To hide column **M** using this method, place the mouse pointer on the column divider between **N** and **M**. Drag the adjust cursor to the left, carefully, until the column width is **0.00**.

ⓘ *Dragging further left hides multiple columns. If this happens, use **Undo** to restore the columns and try again.*

7.　The mouse can also be used to unhide columns or rows. There are two adjust cursors. The normal column adjust cursor is on the left or for a row is above. To the right of a hidden column or below a hidden row the adjust cursor changes to ⁺‖⁺ or ⁼⁺⁼. Dragging this cursor redisplays the hidden data. Unhide column **M** making it **10.00 (75 pixels)** wide.

8.　Close the workbook <u>without</u> saving.

Driving Lesson 14 - Hiding Formulas

▣ Park and Read

The **Hidden** option on the **Protection** tab prevents the cell's contents from being displayed in the **Formula Bar** and is used primarily to hide source formulas (how the results were calculated). The cell contents still display the results.

⌒ Manoeuvres

1. Open the workbook **Invoices**, select the range **F6:F14**.

2. Select **Format | Cells**, then choose the **Protection** tab. Check **Hidden**, then click **OK**.

3. Use **Tools | Protection | Protect Sheet** <u>without</u> a password to turn on the sheet protection.

4. Move the cell pointer into cell **F6**. Notice that the result value is displayed in the cell but the content (formula) is not shown in the **Formula Bar**. **Hidden** prevents the **Formulas** from being viewed even if the resulting values are displayed on the sheet.

	F6	▼	*fx*				
	A	B	C	D	E	F	G
1							
2							
3							
4							
5	Invoice	Date	Co. No.	Company	Amount	VAT	Total
6	156	3-Dec-06	378	Greens	£456.00	£79.80	£535.80
7	164	15-Dec-06	294	Smith & Co	£900.00	£157.50	£1,057.50
8	167	21-Dec-06	345	J Jones	£1,345.00	£235.38	£1,580.38

> **Note:** *Hidden data only hides content from the **Formula Bar**. If it is required to completely hide values in individual cells then change the font colour to match the background colour or hide the whole row/column. This must be done before the worksheet is protected.*

5. To display the formulas again, select **Tools | Protection | Unprotect Sheet**.

6. Select the range **F6:F14**.

7. Select **Format | Cells**, then choose the **Protection** tab. Uncheck **Hidden**, then click **OK**.

8. Click on individual cells in the range **F6:F14** and check that the formulas are displayed in the **Formula Bar**.

9. Close the workbook **Invoices** <u>without</u> saving.

Driving Lesson 15 - Workbook Protection

🅿 Park and Read

Workbooks may contain sensitive or private data which means that the whole workbook has to be kept secure. **Passwords** can be assigned to workbooks so that only those people who know the password can open them.

👉 Manoeuvres

1. Open the workbook **Retail**.

2. Select **File | Save As** then select **Tools | General Options** to display the **Save Options** dialog box.

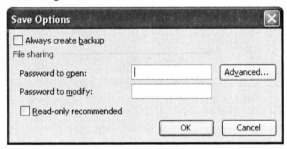

3. In the **Password to open** box, type **PASS** (passwords are case-sensitive. **PASS** is not the same as **pass** or **Pass**). Note that the letters do not appear as you type, only asterisks. Click **OK**.

ℹ️ *Choose a password that is easily remembered, but not so obvious that it can be easily guessed. If passwords are forgotten, the workbook cannot be opened, so the data within all the sheets is lost!*

4. To confirm the password, it must be re-entered. Enter it, then click **OK**.

5. In the **Save As** dialog box, enter **Secure** in the **File name** box, then click **Save**.

6. Close the workbook **Secure** and open it again. A prompt for the password will be displayed.

Driving Lesson 15 - Continued

7. Try typing in an **Incorrect** password and click **OK**. Access is denied.

8. Open the workbook **Secure**, this time enter the correct password, **PASS**. Click **OK**.

9. Workbooks can also be saved with a password to modify added. **Password to modify** allows users who know the password to open, edit and save as normal. Select **File | Save As** then select **Tools | General Options** to display the **Save Options** dialog box.

10. Remove the asterisks from the **Password to open** box and then enter the password **change** in the **Password to modify** box. Click **OK**.

11. Re-enter the password **change** and click **OK**.

12. Click **Save** and then **Yes** to overwrite the previously saved workbook.

13. Close the workbook **Secure**.

14. Users without the password to modify can still open the workbook but as **Read-only**. Any changes made in the workbook mean it has to be saved with a new name, keeping the original unchanged. Open the workbook **Secure**.

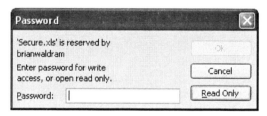

15. The user has a choice to enter the password and proceed normally or as stated, to click the **Read Only** button. Enter the password **change** and click **OK**. The workbook opens with full editing rights.

16. Make a change to any cell in the workbook, save it and then close it.

17. Open the workbook **Secure** and on this occasion click the **Read Only** button. The workbook opens as a read only document. Make a change to the workbook and try and save it with the same name. Click **OK** at the message. Click **Cancel**. Close the workbook <u>without</u> saving the change.

18. Open the workbook **Secure** again, enter the password **change** and click **OK**. To remove the password protection, from the **Save As** dialog box, select **Tools | General Options**. Delete the asterisks in the **Password to modify** box, click **OK** and save the file under the same name, replacing the existing workbook.

19. Close the workbook.

Driving Lesson 16 - Hiding Worksheets & Workbooks

▣ Park and Read

A workbook or a worksheet can be hidden, when the contents are needed but are not to be seen. Hidden worksheets and the workbook still remain open.

⌒ Manoeuvres

1. Open the workbooks **Spires** and **Budget**.

2. With **Budget** as the active workbook select **Window | Hide**. This hides the whole workbook.

3. Check the **Taskbar** for **Budget** and the **Window** menu for open workbooks. **Budget** is not displayed in either.

4. Select **Window | Unhide**.

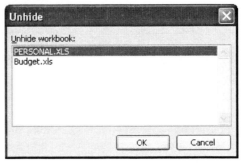

Personal is a workbook that stores global macros, if never used previously it will not be displayed

5. Select **Budget**. Click **OK** to restore it.

6. Make **Spires** active. Click on the **Rates** sheet. This sheet contains the **Tax** and **Vat** rates.

7. Select **Format | Sheet | Hide**. The **Rates** sheet is no longer visible, although the contents are used in the **Accounts** sheet.

8. The sheet is hidden until it is restored. Saving the workbook leaves the sheet hidden. Select **Format | Sheet | Unhide**.

9. Select **Rates**. Click **OK** to restore it.

10. Close the workbooks <u>without</u> saving.

Driving Lesson 17 - Revision: Protection

This is not an ECDL test. Testing may only be carried out through certified ECDL test centres. This covers the features introduced in this section. Try not to refer to the preceding Driving Lessons while completing it.

1. Open the workbook **Easy**. All cells in the worksheet have been **unlocked**.

2. This worksheet stretches from **A1** to **N14**, but has some data hidden. Unhide the data so that the full worksheet is visible.

3. Make the following ranges **locked**:

   B4:M4
   B10:M10
   B14:M14
   N1:N14

4. Add the sheet protection without a password.

5. Enter the **Password to open** as **Pass** and save the workbook as **Protect**.

6. Close the workbook.

7. Open the workbook **Protect**.

8. Remove the workbook password and add the password **007** as a **Password to modify**. Click **Yes** to replace the existing file.

9. Close the workbook.

10. Open the workbook **Protect**, enter the password **007** to be able to modify.

11. Remove the password and save the workbook using the same file name without any password protection. At the prompt to replace the existing file select **Yes**.

12. Close the workbook.

If you experienced any difficulty completing this Revision refer back to the Driving Lessons in this section. Then redo the Revision.

Once you are confident with the features, complete the Record of Achievement Matrix referring to the section at the end of the guide. Only when competent move on to the next Section.

Section 4
Cell Comments

By the end of this Section you should be able to:

Use Cell Comments

Display Comments

Create, Edit and Delete Comments

To gain an understanding of the above features, work through the **Driving Lessons** in this **Section**.

For each **Driving Lesson**, read the **Park and Read** instructions, without touching the keyboard, then work through the numbered steps of the **Manoeuvres** on the computer. Complete the **Revision Exercise(s)** at the end of the section to test your knowledge.

Driving Lesson 18 - Cell Comments

▣ Park and Read

A **Comment** is a piece of text that is attached to a cell. Depending on which options are set, comments are not usually displayed on the worksheet, but a **comment indicator** (a small red triangle) shows where the comments are. They can be easily viewed by moving the mouse pointer over the relevant cell.

⌒ Manoeuvres

1. Open the workbook **Comments**.

2. Some of the cells on the sheet have red triangles in the corners. These cells have comments attached. Place the mouse pointer on cell **D7**, the cell which has a comment indicator (a small red triangle).

3. Leave the mouse pointer over the cell for a while and a box will appear containing the comment for that cell.

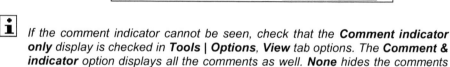

Division	Sales	Profit Employees
North	£11£00	Very impressive sales. Pay a bonus.
South	£97,456	
East	£102,765	
West	£66,833	

ℹ️ *If the comment indicator cannot be seen, check that the* **Comment indicator only** *display is checked in* **Tools | Options**, **View** *tab options. The* **Comment & indicator** *option displays all the comments as well.* **None** *hides the comments and indicators.*

4. Place the mouse over the other cells containing comments in turn and view them.

5. Leave the workbook **Comments** open.

Driving Lesson 19 - Display Comments

▣ Park and Read

Comments can be displayed permanently. The **Reviewing Toolbar** is displayed to manipulate the comments.

☞ Manoeuvres

1. The workbook **Comments** should still be open. If not, open it.

2. Select **View | Comments**. All comments on the active worksheet are shown. The **Reviewing Toolbar** is also displayed.

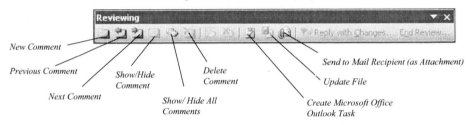

3. The **Show/Hide** button displays or hides all the comments. Click the **Hide All Comments** button, ⬜.

4. To show the **Comments** in turn, the **Next**, 🔲, or **Previous Comment**, 🔲, buttons are used. Click in cell **A1**. Click the **Next Comment** button, 🔲. This displays the **Comment** in **D7** in **Edit** mode.

5. Use the **Next** and **Previous Comment** buttons to scroll from comment to comment. An information message is displayed when the end or beginning of the workbook is reached. Click **OK** if this message is displayed.

6. Click on cell **D7** and click the **Show Comment** button, ⬜. This displays an individual comment. (The same button also hides a displayed comment).

7. Right click on cell **D7** and select **Hide Comment**.

ℹ️ *Comments can be shown or hidden using the **Reviewing Toolbar** (for multiple comments) or the **Shortcut Menu** from a cell (for a single comment).*

8. Close the **Reviewing Toolbar**.

9. Leave the workbook **Comments** open.

Driving Lesson 20 - Create, Edit and Delete Comments

🄿 Park and Read

Comments can be inserted anywhere in a spreadsheet and any text can be added. Text in comments can be edited and comments can be deleted.

℘ Manoeuvres

1. The workbook **Comments** should still be open. If not, open it.

2. To create a comment attached to cell **E10**, right click on **E10** and select **Insert Comment** from the shortcut menu.

ℹ *Alternatively click on the cell and select **Insert | Comment** or click the **New Comment** button ▣, on the **Reviewing Toolbar**.*

3. In the **Comment** box, the user name is added automatically to the top line of the comment, delete it and type **We must improve this figure**.

4. Adjust the size of the **Comment Box** (using the handles). Move the box away from the numbers, by placing the cursor on any edge and clicking and dragging (the cursor changes to a four headed arrow when over the box).

5. Click away from the comment to complete it. The comment indicator is now displayed in the cell **E10**.

6. Move the mouse over cell **E10** to display the **Comment**. The temporary display is next to the cell.

7. Move the mouse on to cell **D7** and display that **Comment**. Right click on cell **D7** and select **Edit Comment**.

ℹ *Alternatively select **Insert | Edit Comment**.*

8. Use the <**Backspace**> key to delete the second sentence and edit the comment to **We cannot afford a bonus**. Reduce the size of the comment box and move it away from the numbers.

9. To remove the note attached to cell **F7**, right click on cell **F7** and select **Delete Comment**. The comment is deleted and the note indicator is removed.

10. Close the workbook **Comments** <u>without</u> saving.

Driving Lesson 21 - Revision: Cell Comments

This is not an ECDL test. Testing may only be carried out through certified ECDL test centres. This covers the features introduced in this section. Try not to refer to the preceding Driving Lessons while completing it.

1. Open the workbook **Budget**.

2. Add the comment **Why the sudden drop in sales?** to cell **J2**.

3. Add the comment **Consider increasing the price** to cell **B3**.

4. Add the comment **Too many employees?** to cell **B5**.

5. Add the comment **This loss needs to be turned into a profit!** to cell **J14**.

6. Using **Page Setup** change the page orientation to **Landscape**, and select **Fit to** one page. Under the **Sheet** tab, select **At end of sheet** for the printed comments. **Print** a copy of the worksheet and the comments.

7. **Show** all the comments on the worksheet.

8. **Hide** the comment attached to cell **J2**.

9. Edit the comment in cell **J14** to read **This loss at the end of year needs to be turned into a profit.**

10. **Delete** the comment attached to cell **B3**.

11. **Hide** all displayed comments.

12. Close the **Reviewing Toolbar**.

13. Close the workbook <u>without</u> saving.

If you experienced any difficulty completing this Revision refer back to the Driving Lessons in this section. Then redo the Revision.

Once you are confident with the features, complete the Record of Achievement Matrix referring to the section at the end of the guide. Only when competent move on to the next Section.

Section 5
Names

By the end of this Section you should be able to:

Use Names

Create and Delete Names for Cell Ranges

Paste and Apply Names

Use Names in Formulas

Use Names with Go To

To gain an understanding of the above features, work through the **Driving Lessons** in this **Section**.

For each **Driving Lesson**, read the **Park and Read** instructions, without touching the keyboard, then work through the numbered steps of the **Manoeuvres** on the computer. Complete the **Revision Exercise(s)** at the end of the section to test your knowledge.

Driving Lesson 22 - Names

◫ Park and Read

Names can be used to represent the contents of a cell or a range of cells to make referencing them easier.

Formulas use cell addresses, e.g. **F37**; these have to be traced back to see what they represent. For example, a formula might be **=D34-D67**, where **D34** represents **Income** and **D67** represents **Expenditure**. Using **Names** the same formula would be:

= Income - Expenditure

making it easier for anyone viewing the formula to understand what it is.

Any cell or range in a worksheet can be given a name by using the **Insert | Name | Define** command or by typing directly into the **Name Box**. For this name to be used as a reference in formulas, the command **Insert | Name | Apply** must be used.

☞ Manoeuvres

1.   Open the workbook **Vat**.

2.   In **C6** enter the formula to calculate the **VAT**. Remember, this will have to use **Absolute Addressing**. The formula is **=C5*$B$15**.

3.   Copy this formula across the row into **D6** and **E6**. Complete the **Total Price** row, adding the **Price** to the **VAT**.

4.   Click on cell **B15**, the **VAT Rate**. Enter the new rate of **17.5%** (include the **%** sign).

5.   The use of **Names** would make the formulas in this worksheet easier to understand. Click on cell **B15** and select **Insert | Name | Define**.

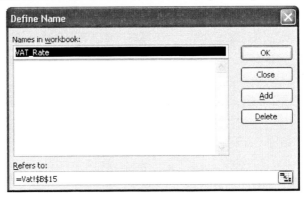

Driving Lesson 22 - Continued

6. The **Define Name** dialog box shows any **Names** already defined in the workbook (none in this case) and may suggest a name for the selected cell (**VAT_Rate**). It also displays where the name **Refers to** (Vat!$B$15). The suggested name may be overwritten, but as **VAT_Rate** is a suitable name, click on **Add** to add this name to the worksheet, then click on **OK**.

i *Define **Names** picks its suggestions from any nearby labels but replaces spaces with underscores as spaces are not allowed in **Names**. If there are no suitable suggestions the **Name** box will be blank.*

7. Note that the **Name Box** (above the column **A** heading) now contains the name of the cell, **VAT_Rate**. Move to cell **C6**. The cell contents still reference **$B$15**. The cell has been named but not used anywhere yet.

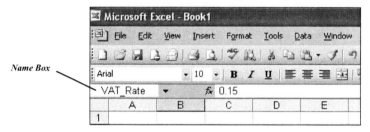

8. Select **Insert | Name | Apply**. There is a list of available names, in this case just **VAT_Rate**. Click on **OK** to apply this name to the worksheet.

9. Note that the reference for **C6** now says **C5*VAT_Rate**. The other **VAT** cells are similar.

10. Cells and ranges can also be named by selecting the required cell/s and then typing directly into the **Name Box**. Select the range **C5:E5** and type the name **Price** in the **Name Box** and press <**Enter**> to complete the naming process.

11. Click away from the range and click the **Name Box** drop down and select **Price**, the named range **C5:E5** is highlighted.

i *Single cells can be named and used in exactly the same way.*

12. Save the workbook as **Vat2**.

13. Leave the workbook open for the next Driving Lesson.

Driving Lesson 23 - Using Names in Formulas

▣ Park and Read

As well as manually defining **Names** for cells, **Names** can be automatically created for ranges of cells based on existing row and column headers using the **Insert | Name | Create** command.

Existing **Names** can be used in new formulas by typing the cell name or by using the **Insert | Name | Paste** command.

◔ Manoeuvres

1. Open the workbook **Vat2** if it is not already open.

2. Select the range **B4:E7**.

3. Select **Insert | Name | Create** to display the **Create Names** dialog box.

4. Make sure **Top Row** and **Left Column** are selected. Click **OK** to create names based on the row and column headers for the selected range.

5. Select **Insert | Name | Apply** to display all the names just created. The new names should be highlighted. Click **OK** to apply these names to all formulas.

6. Select **C7** to see names used in the formula rather than cell references. Look at other cells containing formulas.

7. Insert a column between **March** and **Total**. In **F4** enter **April** and in **F5** type **5050**.

8. In **F6** type **=F5*** and then select **Insert | Name | Paste**.

9. Click on **VAT_Rate** in the **Paste Name** list, then **OK**. The name is pasted into the formula. Press **<Enter>** to complete the formula.

10. Enter the appropriate formula in **F7** to add the **Total Price** for April. Note that as **Column F** was added after creating the names it is not included in the named ranges.

ℹ️ *To include names in the new column, the names have to be redefined. It is better to leave the creating and applying of names until after the spreadsheet structure has been completed.*

11. Change the formulas in the **Total** column to include the new figures.

12. Save the workbook **Vat2** and leave it open for the next Driving Lesson.

Driving Lesson 24 - Using Go To with Names

▣ Park and Read

The **Go To** command can not only be used to move quickly to a cell by typing its reference, but also to move to any named cell or range.

ℝ Manoeuvres

1. Open the workbook **Vat2** if it is not already open.

2. Select **Edit | Go To**.

 *Alternatively the key press <**Ctrl G**> or the function key <**F5**> can be used.*

3. All the names on the sheet are listed. Click **VAT_Rate** and then **OK**.

4. The cell containing the **VAT_Rate**, i.e. **B15**, is now the active cell.

5. Press <**F5**>, the **Go To** key. Select **January** from the list and click **OK**. The range of cells named **January** is highlighted.

6. Close the workbook <u>without</u> saving.

7. Open the workbook **Accounts**.

8. Press <**F5**>, the **Go To** key. There is a long list of all the named ranges in this sheet. Select **Materials** then **OK**. The range containing the **Materials** figures will be highlighted. Use the horizontal scroll bar to view the whole range if necessary.

9. Select **Edit | Go To**, choose **Budget** and click **OK**. The figures for the whole spreadsheet are now highlighted.

10. This named range is now not required, to delete it select **Insert | Name | Define**.

11. Click on **Budget** in the list and then click **Delete**.

12. Click **OK** to complete the removal of the range name.

13. Select **Edit | Go To** and check the list for **Budget**. The name has been deleted. Click **Cancel**.

14. Close the workbook <u>without</u> saving.

Driving Lesson 25 - Revision: Names

This is not an ECDL test. Testing may only be carried out through certified ECDL test centres. This covers the features introduced in this section. Try not to refer to the preceding Driving Lessons while completing it.

1.   Open the workbook **Retail**.

2.   **Create** names for the whole worksheet, i.e. **A1:N14.**

3.   **Apply** the names you have just created.

4.   Move to cell **P3** and type **=Sales Feb** to find the sales figure for **February**.

5.   Similarly, find the amount of **Spending** in **April (Apr)**.

6.   **Go To** the **Sales** figures and format the named range as **bold**.

7.   Close the workbook <u>without</u> saving.

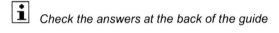 *Check the answers at the back of the guide*

If you experienced any difficulty completing this Revision refer back to the Driving Lessons in this section. Then redo the Revision.

Once you are confident with the features, complete the Record of Achievement Matrix referring to the section at the end of the guide. Only when competent move on to the next Section.

Section 6
Templates

By the end of this Section you should be able to:

Create and Understand Templates

Use Templates

Edit Templates

To gain an understanding of the above features, work through the **Driving Lessons** in this **Section**.

For each **Driving Lesson**, read the **Park and Read** instructions, without touching the keyboard, then work through the numbered steps of the **Manoeuvres** on the computer. Complete the **Revision Exercise(s)** at the end of the section to test your knowledge.

Driving Lesson 26 - Creating a Template

▣ Park and Read

A **Template** is a base worksheet that has been prepared ready for data to be entered. It can contain: text, graphics, formulas, protection, macros and formatting. Using a template ensures consistency of appearance and performance for the spreadsheets based on it.

Templates are created by specifying a **Save as type** of **Template** when saving. They are given a file extension of **.xlt** which distinguishes them from normal workbooks.

⌒ Manoeuvres

1. Open the workbook **Budget**. This represents the budget data for a small company.

2. To change this workbook into a template, the base data must be removed, leaving the formulas. Delete the data in the ranges **B2:M3**, **B5:M6** and **B8:M9**.

3. To save this workbook as a **Template**, select **File | Save As**.

4. In **Save as type**, choose **Template**.

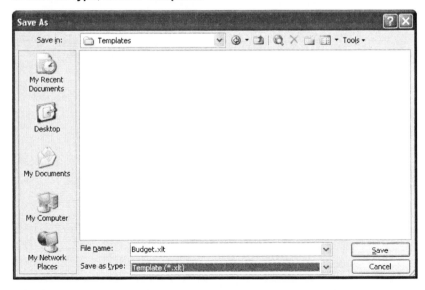

5. Notice how **Save in** changes. Click **Save**. The workbook is then saved as a template and stored with other templates in the **Templates** folder.

6. Close the **Budget** template.

Driving Lesson 27 - Using a Template

⊞ Park and Read

A template can be opened repeatedly and used as the base for many other spreadsheets. These are saved as workbooks with new names to leave the original template unaffected.

⌒ Manoeuvres

1.   To use a template, select **File | New**.

2.   The **New Workbook** task pane is displayed. Under **Templates**, click **On my computer** to view the **Templates** dialog box.

3.   The **General** tab is displayed by default including the **Budget.xlt** template.

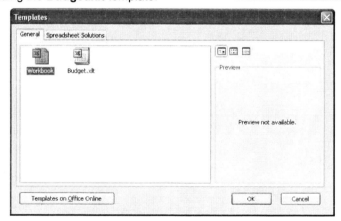

4.   Click on the **Spreadsheet Solutions** tab to view other pre-designed templates. *Excel* has several preloaded templates ready for personalisation.

5.   Select the **General** tab again, click on **Budget** and then **OK**. A workbook, **Budget1**, is opened based on the **template**. Data can now be added. Add some data to column **B** to see if the formulas work.

6.   The name **Budget1** is similar in use to the default workbook names **Book1**, etc. To save the template as a workbook, select **File | Save** or click the **Save** button, to display the **Save As** dialog box.

7.   Save the workbook as **Budget2** (take care to save to the required location not the **Templates** folder).

8.   Start a new workbook based on the **Budget** template and view both open workbooks using the **Window** command. Close both the workbooks <u>without</u> saving.

Driving Lesson 28 - Editing a Template

▣ Park and Read

If required, templates can be resaved as templates with the same file name, allowing the original template to be overwritten to incorporate changes.

☞ Manoeuvres

1. Start a new workbook based on the **Budget** template.

2. Change the tax rate to **40**%.

3. Change the orientation of the page to landscape and ensure that the spreadsheet fits onto one page.

4. Format the numbers within rows **2 to 4**, **6 to 11**, **13 & 14** as currency with 2 decimal places.

5. To resave the workbook as the same template, select **File | Save As**.

6. Change the **Save as type** to **Template (*.xlt)** and enter the file name **Budget**.

7. Click **Save**.

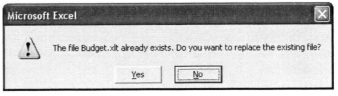

8. A dialog box appears informing that the **Budget** file already exists, click **Yes** to overwrite the original template. Close the **Budget** template.

9. Open a copy of the template to check that the changes have been made.

10. Close all open workbooks.

11. The templates are stored on the **C:** drive. The created **template** is to be deleted. Select **File | New**.

12. In the **Task Pane** click **On my computer**. The templates are displayed with 🗒 icons (a yellow stripe along the top of a pad of pages). Right click on **Budget.xlt** and from the shortcut menu select **Delete**. Click **Yes** to confirm the deletion and **Cancel** the dialog box.

13. Display the **Templates** dialog box to check that the template has been successfully deleted.

14. Click **Cancel** to close the **Templates** dialog box.

Driving Lesson 29 - Revision: Templates

This is not an ECDL test. Testing may only be carried out through certified ECDL test centres. This covers the features introduced in this section. Try not to refer to the preceding Driving Lessons while completing it.

1. Open the workbook **Retail** and delete all the values on rows **2**, **3** and **5** to **9**.

2. Save the workbook as a **Template**, using the same name and close it.

3. Open a new workbook based on the **Retail** template.

4. To add data to the template, open the workbook **Retail Data**.

5. Copy and paste the data in range **A3:L4** from **Retail Data** to **B2** in **Retail1** and the range **A6:L10** to **B5**.

6. Save the workbook to the data folder as **Retail2**.

7. Close the workbook. Close **Retail Data**.

8. The **Retail** template is to be deleted. Select **File | New** and click **On my computer**.

9. Right click on the **Retail** template and select **Delete**.

10. Click **Yes** to confirm the deletion.

11. Check that the template **Retail** has been deleted.

12. Click **Cancel** to close the **Templates** dialog box.

13. Close the **New Workbook** task pane.

If you experienced any difficulty completing this Revision refer back to the Driving Lessons in this section. Then redo the Revision.

Once you are confident with the features, complete the Record of Achievement Matrix referring to the section at the end of the guide. Only when competent move on to the next Section.

Section 7
Formulas

By the end of this Section you should be able to:

Display and Check Formulas

Understand Formulas that Produce Errors

Use Mixed Cell Referencing

Create Custom Number Formats

To gain an understanding of the above features, work through the **Driving Lessons** in this **Section**.

For each **Driving Lesson**, read the **Park and Read** instructions, without touching the keyboard, then work through the numbered steps of the **Manoeuvres** on the computer. Complete the **Revision Exercise(s)** at the end of the section to test your knowledge.

Driving Lesson 30 - Display Formulas

▣ Park and Read

It is sometimes useful to identify quickly which cells within a worksheet are formulas rather than entered data, and to display the actual formulas on the screen instead of the results. This is particularly relevant when checking whether all formulas are correct. Individual formulas can also be displayed in a way that aids checking.

ℝ Manoeuvres

1.   Open the workbook **Balance**.

2.   To determine which cells in the worksheet are formulas, select **Edit | Go To** and click the **Special** button.

3.   Select **Formulas** and click **OK**. All formula cells are selected, showing for example that the **Charities** values are not simply entered numbers but calculations.

4.   To display all the formulas on a worksheet the key press combination <Ctrl `> is used. Press the **Ctrl** and the key under the **Esc** key. All formulas will be shown in full, the columns being widened where necessary.

i *The* ***Formula Auditing*** *toolbar may also be displayed.*

5.   Press < **Ctrl** `> again to revert to the normal view (results rather than formulas).

i *Alternatively all formulas may be displayed by selecting* ***Tools | Options****, selecting the* ***View*** *tab and checking the* ***Formulas*** *box under* ***Window options****.*

6.   Ensure that the worksheet is in normal view and double click on cell **D16**. The formula is displayed in the cell itself with colour coding to show which cells or ranges are used in the formula. So the reference to **C16** is in blue and the cell **C16** is outlined in blue.

7.   The worksheet is in **In-cell edit** mode now so that the formula can be amended, by dragging the coloured outlines to different cells or by dragging the **Fill Handle** to extend the range. After checking, press <Enter> (to accept any changes) or <Esc> (to reject any changes) to finish the editing.

8.   Leave the workbook **Balance** open.

Driving Lesson 31 - Formulas that Produce Errors

▣ Park and Read

There can be problems when some formulas are calculated, usually because the referenced cells are not as expected. When a formula cannot be calculated the cell displays an error message. Functions **ISERROR** and **ERROR.TYPE** can be used to check for and identify errors.

The following error values (with their error type number) can be found:

#NULL!	1	The two areas specified do not intersect
#DIV/0!	2	Division by zero
#VALUE!	3	The wrong argument used
#REF!	4	Cell referenced is not valid
#NAME?	5	Does not recognise text in a formula
#NUM!	6	Error with number in formula
#N/A	7	The value used in the formula is not available
######		The result is too long to fit into the cell

↱ Manoeuvres

1.   The workbook **Balance** should still be open. If not, open it.

2.   In cell **H20** enter the function **=ISERROR(H18)** to check whether the formula in **H18** is producing an error. It should read **FALSE**.

3.   In cell **H4**, enter the number **0**. Cell **H18** is now a **#DIV/0!** error because it is trying to divide by **H4**. **H20** should read **TRUE**.

4.   Cell **H18** is displayed with a green triangle. Click on cell **H18**, a **Smart Tag** is displayed, ⬦.

5.   Click on the tag to display a list of options.

6.   The error is shown as a **Divide by Zero Error**. Investigate the available options.

7.   Using the function **IF** can replace errors with a specific value. In cell **H18** enter the formula **=IF(H4=0,0,H16/H4)**. If **H4** is zero the formula is not calculated (so no error and **H20** = **FALSE** again) and the value of **0** is returned.

8.   In cell **H4**, enter the character **X**. Cells **H16** and **H18** are now **#VALUE!** errors because both expect cell **H4** to be a numeric value.

9.   In cell **J20** enter the function **=ERROR.TYPE(H18)** to identify any error in cell **H18**. The result is error type **3**.

10. Close the workbook <u>without</u> saving.

Driving Lesson 32 - Mixed Referencing

▣ Park and Read

Mixed Referencing is a cross between **Absolute** and **Relative**. One part of the reference is fixed with a **$** symbol and the other part is not, e.g. **$A15** (column **A** fixed) or **A$15** (row **15** fixed).

Manoeuvres

1. Start a new workbook.

2. Create the following spreadsheet.

	A	B	C	D	E	F	G
1							
2		10%	20%	30%	40%	50%	
3	5						
4	10						
5	15						
6	20						
7	25						
8							

3. In cell **B3** enter the formula **=A3*B2**, to calculate **10%** of **5**.

4. Use the **Fill Handle** to drag the formula across to **F3**.

5. With the range still highlighted, drag the **Fill Handle** down to row **7** to fill the rest of the range.

	A	B	C	D	E	F	G
1							
2		10%	20%	30%	40%	50%	
3	5	0.5	0.1	0.03	0.012	0.006	
4	10	5	0.5	0.015	0.00018	1.08E-06	
5	15	75	37.5	0.5625	0.000101	1.09E-10	
6	20	1500	56250	31640.63	3.203613	3.5E-10	
7	25	37500	2.11E+09	6.67E+13	2.14E+14	74902.76	
8							
9							

6. Double click on cell **D5** to check the formula and which cells it uses. The formula is **=C5*D4** because of **Relative Addressing**.

7. The formula should be **=A5*D2**. Highlight and delete the range **B3:F7**.

8. Try and use **Absolute Referencing** to overcome this problem. In cell **B3** type the formula **=$A$3*$B$2**.

Driving Lesson 32 - Continued

9. Drag this formula across to column **F** and then down to row **7**.

10. Double click on cell **D5** to check the formulas and which cells it uses. The formula is **=$A$3*$B$2**, so all of the formulas are now the same, which is not correct.

	A	B	C	D	E	F	G
1							
2		10%	20%	30%	40%	50%	
3	5	0.5	0.5	0.5	0.5	0.5	
4	10	0.5	0.5	0.5	0.5	0.5	
5	15	0.5	0.5	=$A$3*$B$2		0.5	
6	20	0.5	0.5	0.5	0.5	0.5	
7	25	0.5	0.5	0.5	0.5	0.5	
8							

11. **Mixed Referencing** can be used to fix the column as **A** and row as **2**, allowing the other reference to change, to calculate the formulas.

12. Highlight, then delete the range **B3:F7** again and move back to cell **B3**.

13. Type the formula **=$A3*B$2**, this fixes column **A** and row **2** because the **dollar** signs are before these values in the formula.

14. Drag this new formula across to **F3** and then down to row **7**.

	A	B	C	D	E	F	G
1							
2		10%	20%	30%	40%	50%	
3	5	0.5	1	1.5	2	2.5	
4	10	1	2	3	4	5	
5	15	1.5	3	4.5	6	7.5	
6	20	2	4	6	8	10	
7	25	2.5	5	7.5	10	12.5	
8							
9							

15. Double click in cell **D5** and check that the formula is **=$A5*D$2**.

	A	B	C	D	E	F	G
1							
2		10%	20%	30%	40%	50%	
3	5	0.5	1	1.5	2	2.5	
4	10	1	2	3	4	5	
5	15	1.5	3	=$A5*D$2	6	7.5	
6	20	2	4	6	8	10	
7	25	2.5	5	7.5	10	12.5	
8							

16. Save the workbook as **Mixed**.

17. Close the workbook.

Driving Lesson 33 - Custom Number Formats

▣ Park and Read

As well as formatting cells using the standard number categories such as **Currency** and **Date**, it is possible to create **Custom** formats using a variety of codes. Some of the available codes are listed below:

d	day number without leading zero, e.g. 5
dd	day number with leading zero, e.g. 05
ddd	day abbreviated as text, e.g. Mon
dddd	day as text, e.g. Monday
m	month without leading zero, e.g. 6 (if used after hh Excel assumes minutes)
mm	month with leading zero, e.g. 06
mmm	month abbreviated as text, e.g. Jun
mmmm	month as text, e.g. September
h	hours without leading zero based on 24 hour clock unless used with am/pm
hh	hours with leading zero based on 24 hour clock unless used with am/pm
[colour]	displays whatever is following in the stated colour Black, Cyan, Magenta, Blue, White, Green, Red and Yellow.
[condition value]	where condition may be <, >, =, >=, <=, <> and value can be any number
#	displays only significant digits
0	displays insignificant zeros
?	adds spaces either side of decimal point
,	thousands separator
.	decimal separator

↻ Manoeuvres

1. Start a new workbook. In cell **B2** enter **56**. Click back on cell **B2** and select **Format | Cells**.

2. Select the **Number** tab if not already selected.

3. The normal formatting is achieved by using the standard categories of **General**, **Number**, **Currency**, **Percentage**, etc. Click on **Custom** to display the list from which to select and optionally amend.

Driving Lesson 33 - Continued

4. The **Type** box is where the custom format is created. Scroll down the list of built-in **Types**. Select one and check how it affects the display in the **Sample** box.

5. Select the third item in the list **0.00**, edit this in the **Type** box to display just one decimal place, remove one of the zeros. Click **OK**.

The built-in format used as a starting point for a custom format is still unchanged and available to use.

6. In cell **B4** press **<Ctrl ;>** to enter today's date, press **<Enter>**. Click on cell **B4** and select **Format | Cells** and click the **Custom** category.

7. To create a custom date, select a date format to work from, choose **dd-mmm-yy**. Edit this in the **Type** box to read **ddd dd mmmm yyyy**.

Sample
Thu 08 January 2009

Type:

ddd dd mmmm yyyy|
##0.0E+0
?/?
??/??
dd/mm/yyyy
dd-mmm-yy
dd-mmm
mmm-yy

8. Check the **Sample** box and click **OK**. Column **B** is widened to display the date.

9. Enter your birth date in cell **B6** in the form **dd/mm/yyyy**.

10. **Format** this date using the **Custom** date format already created, the **Custom Formats** are stored at the end of the list. This displays the day as well as the date on which you were born.

11. Close the workbook <u>without</u> saving.

Driving Lesson 34 - Revision: Formulas

This is not an ECDL test. Testing may only be carried out through certified ECDL test centres. This covers the features introduced in this section. Try not to refer to the preceding Driving Lessons while completing it.

1.   Open the workbook **Errors**. This workbook contains a variety of faults, some of which are incorrect ranges in functions that are not shown as errors.

2.   Correct any errors that are contained in any of the formulas. For the division by zero error, replace the formulas in that column with an **IF** statement that replaces the error with zero when it occurs.

3.   Format the range **J4:K10** with a custom number format to display percentages with one decimal place.

4.   In the range **C3:G3** enter the actual dates for last week. Format the range **C3:G3** with custom dates to display a **2** digit day, followed by a - then a two digit month, e.g. 03-05 for May 3rd.

5.   The range **B4:B9** contains employee numbers. Some contain 3 digits, some 4 and some 5. Use a custom number format on the range so that all the numbers are **6** digits (use the format **000000**) to add the leading zeros.

6.   Check cell **K10**, it should be **100.0%** if the formulas are correct.

7.   Print a copy of the worksheet.

8.   Close the workbook <u>without</u> saving.

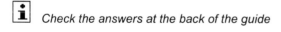

Check the answers at the back of the guide

If you experienced any difficulty completing this Revision refer back to the Driving Lessons in this section. Then redo the Revision.

Once you are confident with the features, complete the Record of Achievement Matrix referring to the section at the end of the guide. Only when competent move on to the next Section.

Section 8
Outlines

By the end of this Section you should be able to:

Create an Outline

Expand and Collapse Outline Level Details

To gain an understanding of the above features, work through the **Driving Lessons** in this **Section**.

For each **Driving Lesson**, read the **Park and Read** instructions, without touching the keyboard, then work through the numbered steps of the **Manoeuvres** on the computer. Complete the **Revision Exercise(s)** at the end of the section to test your knowledge.

Driving Lesson 35 - Creating an Outline

🅿 Park and Read

An **Outline** is used to hide parts of a worksheet, making it easier to see the more important areas. Different users may need to see different information or different amounts of information.

An outline can show up to eight different **levels**, both horizontally and vertically, with each level showing a different amount of data. The levels are **displayed** or **hidden** to show the required data.

🗘 Manoeuvres

1.   Open the workbook **House**.

2.   Select **Data | Group and Outline | Auto Outline**. *Excel* assumes that the summary rows (the formulas) are at the bottom of the detail and the summary columns are to the right.

Level Buttons

Row Level Bars

Hide Buttons

	A	B	C	D	E	F	G	H	I
	A1		ƒ	House Finance					
1	**House Finance**	Jan	Feb	Mar	Apr	May	Jun	Jul	Aug
2	Pay	1185	1185	1185	1250	1250	1250	1250	1250
3	Other Income	0	0	0	0	0	0	0	0
4	Total Income	1185	1185	1185	1250	1250	1250	1250	1250
5	Rent	200	200	200	200	200	200	200	220
6	Holidays	0	0	0	500	0	0	0	3000
7	Leisure	125	200	175	100	50	120	56	180
8	Electricity	89	0	0	140	0	0	80	0
9	Gas	150	0	0	200	0	0	120	0
10	Telephone	0	76	0	0	83	0	0	93
11	Car	0	56	291	0	0	67	0	0
12	Petrol	60	75	60	75	75	60	60	50
13	Food	240	260	200	240	220	240	230	240
14	Others	55	45	100	65	75	150	100	75
15	Total Expenses	919	912	1026	1520	703	837	846	3858
16	Savings	266	539	698	428	975	1388	1792	-816
17									

3.   The outline has been created. It has 3 row levels and 2 column levels. Notice the various buttons and bars above and to the left of the worksheet.

4.   The **Hide** detail symbol ▣, hides rows or columns in an outline level when clicked. Click the **Hide** button next to **Row 15** to hide rows 5 to 14.

5.   The **Show** detail symbol ⊞, indicates hidden rows or columns. Click on the button, ⊞, next to **Row 15** to expand the hidden rows.

Driving Lesson 35 - Continued

6. Row and column level buttons, $\boxed{1}\ \boxed{2}\ \boxed{3}$, indicate the number of levels in an outline. Click on them to display a specific level - the lower the number, the less detail is displayed. Click on row level **1** and column level **1**.

7. Click on the row level **3** button and the column level **2** button to fully expand the **Outline**.

8. The row and column level bars indicate the range of data in a level. Click on them to hide the data, as an alternative to using the **Hide** detail button. Click on the detail level bar across the columns to hide the columns **B** to **M**.

9. Expand the columns to full view using any method.

10. To remove the **Auto Outline**, select **Data | Group and Outline | Clear Outline**. The outline is removed.

11. Close the workbook <u>without</u> saving.

Driving Lesson 36 - Working with an Outline

Park and Read

Outlines are used to restrict the amount of data seen on a worksheet. When an outline is created, the levels appear around summary rows and columns, as these are usually the most important areas of a worksheet. Levels can be expanded and collapsed using the buttons described in the last exercise.

Manoeuvres

1. Open the workbook **Retail**.

2. Add an **Auto Outline** to the worksheet by selecting **Data | Group and Outline | Auto Outline**.

3. The outline is fully expanded. It has 4 row levels and 2 column levels. Hide the first row level by clicking on the row level button **3**. This is one level down.

4. Hide the rows by clicking on the **Hide Detail** symbol, ⊟, for the **first** level. The worksheet now only shows three rows.

5. Hide the columns by clicking on the column level button **1**. The worksheet is now fully collapsed, showing only **Tax** and **Net Profit**.

6. Display the rows to the **third** level by clicking on the row level button **3**.

7. Click on the **Hide detail** symbol next to row **11** to hide the **Turnover** and **Spending** rows.

8. Practise showing and hiding levels using the ⊞ and ⊟ symbols.

9. Remove the outline by selecting **Data | Group and Outline | Clear Outline**. The outline is removed.

10. Rows and columns can be highlighted and an outline added manually if the **Auto Outline** is not satisfactory. Highlight rows **2** and **3**, then select **Data | Group and Outline | Group** to add an outline level to row **4**.

11. Highlight rows **5** to **9** and group them to add an outline.

12. Highlight rows **2** to **13** and group them to add another outline level.

Driving Lesson 36 - Continued

13. Highlight columns **B** to **M** and group them to add a horizontal outline. An **Outline** has now been manually created with 3 row levels and 2 column levels, as shown below:

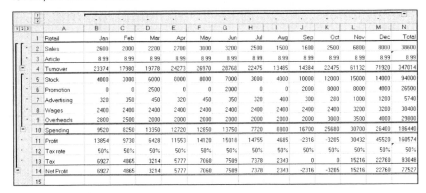

14. Collapse all the levels.

15. Expand all the levels and highlight rows **2** and **3**, then select **Data | Group and Outline | Ungroup** to remove a part of the **Outline**.

16. To remove the whole outline, click on any cell and select **Data | Group and Outline | Clear Outline**.

17. Close the workbook <u>without</u> saving.

Driving Lesson 37 - Revision: Outlines

This is not an ECDL test. Testing may only be carried out through certified ECDL test centres. This covers the features introduced in this section. Try not to refer to the preceding Driving Lessons while completing it.

1. Open the workbook **Spires**.

2. Add an **Auto Outline** to the worksheet.

3. Display the row level **3**.

4. Set the display to **Landscape** and fit to one page.

5. Obtain a printed copy.

6. Remove the **Auto Outline**.

7. Create a manual outline by grouping rows **4** to **13** and rows **18** to **29**.

8. Collapse the rows.

9. Print a copy of the outlined worksheet.

10. Remove the **Outline** on rows **4** to **13**.

11. Close the workbook <u>without</u> saving.

If you experienced any difficulty completing this Revision refer back to the Driving Lessons in this section. Then redo the Revision.

Once you are confident with the features, complete the Record of Achievement Matrix referring to the section at the end of the guide. Only when competent move on to the next Section.

Section 9
Scenarios

By the end of this Section you should be able to:

Create Scenarios

Use, Edit and Delete Scenarios

Create Scenario Summary Reports

To gain an understanding of the above features, work through the **Driving Lessons** in this **Section**.

For each **Driving Lesson**, read the **Park and Read** instructions, without touching the keyboard, then work through the numbered steps of the **Manoeuvres** on the computer. Complete the **Revision Exercise(s)** at the end of the section to test your knowledge.

Driving Lesson 38 - Creating Scenarios

▣ Park and Read

When a worksheet is used as a model, certain key input values are varied to see the effect on the resulting solutions. Separate versions of the worksheet, showing different input values and solutions, can be saved as **Scenarios**. This helps in "What-If?" situations, where various solutions can be named and be displayed to compare, for example, the best and worst cases.

⌁ Manoeuvres

1. Open the workbook **Food**, which shows the ingredients available to make 3 products and the profit from each product. Different mixes of production will produce different total profit. Ensure that the cells **F5:H5** are all **0**.

2. Highlight the range **F5:H5** and select **Tools | Scenarios**, then click **Add**.

3. Enter the **Scenario** name as **Worst**. Make sure the **Changing cells** are **F5:H5**, then click **OK**.

4. Leave the values of the three changing cells as **0** and click **OK**. **Worst** is now displayed in the **Scenario** list.

5. The next scenario will be a guess to try and maximise the profit. Click **Add**, enter the name as **Guess** and click **OK**. Enter the values of the 3 cells as **100, 120** and **110**.

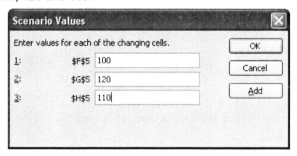

6. Click **OK**. Click **Show** to see the results with these values.

7. The next scenario will be another guess to try and maximise the profit. Click **Add**, enter the name as **Guess2** and click **OK**. Enter the values of the 3 cells as **150, 150** and **160**. Click **OK**.

8. Click **Add** again, enter the name as **Best** and click **OK**. This **Scenario** will use figures that have been calculated elsewhere (using **Solver** – which is not included as part of this syllabus) to produce the best possible value of **Profit, G17**. Enter the values of the cells as **159, 167** and **200**. Click **OK**.

9. Click on **Close**. Four scenarios have now been created. Save the workbook as **Scenario** and leave it open.

Driving Lesson 39 - Using, Editing and Deleting Scenarios

🅿 Park and Read

Once **Scenarios** have been created, they can be viewed by selecting the required scenario from the list. **Scenarios** can also be edited and deleted using the **Scenario Manager** dialog box.

🧭 Manoeuvres

1. The workbook **Scenario** should still be open. If not, open it.

2. Select **Tools | Scenarios**. The four scenarios created in the last Driving Lesson are displayed in the list.

3. The scenario **Guess2** is not wanted, to delete it, click on **Guess2** and then click **Delete**. The **Guess2** scenario is removed from the list.

4. Select **Guess** then select **Show** (the dialog box may have to be moved to see the values on the worksheet). The values and the solution for the **Guess** scenario are now displayed.

5. Show the **Best** scenario.

6. Show the **Worst** scenario, click **Edit** and **OK**. The worst scenario can now be changed. Change the values so that they are all **50**. Click on **OK**.

7. **Close** the **Scenario Manager** dialog box.

8. Save the workbook using the same name and leave the workbook open.

Driving Lesson 40 - Scenario Summary Report

▣ Park and Read

A **Scenario Summary Report** is a report that lists all the scenarios created on a worksheet, along with the **result cells**.

☞ Manoeuvres

1. The workbook **Scenario** should still be open. If not, open it.

2. Select **Tools | Scenarios**. Click on **Summary**.

3. The **Result cell** is the **Total Profit**, **G17**. Click on the cell **G17**. Move the dialog box if necessary.

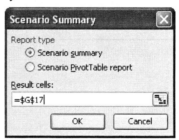

4. Click **OK**. The **Summary Report** is now displayed.

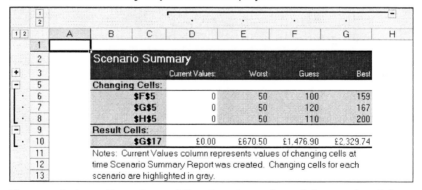

5. The report shows the values of the changing cells and the result cell for each scenario. An **outline view**, is provided, allowing certain rows and columns to be grouped or un-grouped. The outline can be manipulated to change the view of the data. The details of this process are covered in the **Adding Sub Totals** Driving Lesson.

6. The report is created on a separate sheet called **Scenario Summary** within the current workbook.

7. Save the workbook using the same name and then close the workbook.

Driving Lesson 41 - Revision: Scenarios

This is not an ECDL test. Testing may only be carried out through certified ECDL test centres. This covers the features introduced in this section. Try not to refer to the preceding Driving Lessons while completing it.

1. Open the workbook **Mailshot**.

2. The range **C7:C9** should be empty, if not delete the contents of the range.

3. Display the **Scenario Manager** and add the scenario: **Guess1** with the values for **C7:C9** as **800**, **700** and **500**.

4. Add the scenario: **Guess2** with the values for **C7:C9** as **1000**, **600** and **400**.

5. Add the scenario: **Guess3** with the values for **C7:C9** as **750**, **750** and **500**.

6. The three **Scenarios** are now named. Show the results for **Guess2** and print a copy of the worksheet.

7. Use the **Scenario Manager** to produce a **Scenario Summary**, the **Result Cell** is **I11**.

8. Print a copy of the **Scenario Summary**.

9. Use **Tools | Scenario | Delete** to delete the Scenario **Guess3**.

10. Save the workbook as **Mailshot Scenarios**.

11. Close the workbook.

If you experienced any difficulty completing this Revision refer back to the Driving Lessons in this section. Then redo the Revision.

Once you are confident with the features, complete the Record of Achievement Matrix referring to the section at the end of the guide. Only when competent move on to the next Section.

Section 10
Linking & Importing

By the end of this Section you should be able to:

Link Cells

Link between Worksheets and Workbooks

Link to a Word Document

Use Hyperlinks

Importing Delimited Data

Consolidate using 3D-Sum

To gain an understanding of the above features, work through the **Driving Lessons** in this **Section**.

For each **Driving Lesson**, read the **Park and Read** instructions, without touching the keyboard, then work through the numbered steps of the **Manoeuvres** on the computer. Complete the **Revision Exercise(s)** at the end of the section to test your knowledge.

Driving Lesson 42 - Linking

🅿 Park and Read

A link is a formula reference to a cell in the same sheet, another sheet in the same workbook or to another workbook. The sheet that contains the link is called the **container** workbook. The workbook pointed to by the link, which has the original data, is known as the **source** workbook. The reference is **live**, which means that if all sheets are open, any changes in the source workbook are automatically seen in the container workbook.

Links can be used to consolidate several related worksheets/workbooks into one. For example, information from several sources can be gathered together into one workbook to show the overall company results from all the divisions.

To create links between workbooks or other applications, the source application must support **DDE** (Dynamic Data Exchange) or **OLE** (Object Linking and Embedding).

Linking data has a number of advantages:

- To share information
- To simplify a complex problem by breaking it down into several separate workbooks
- To divide work among several people
- To build models normally too large for memory
- To add flexibility to workbooks

🐎 Manoeuvres

1. Open the workbook **Link Demo** and display the **Consol** sheet. This represents the consolidated results for a Company with 3 regions.

2. Click on **C8**. The formula contains a reference to cell **C7** so that if **C7** changes, so will **C8**. This is the simplest form of link.

3. The range **C6** to **F7** contains references like **South!C6**. This is a link referring to the cell **C6** on sheet **South**.

4. Note the profit figure for the **Fourth Quarter,** then switch to the worksheet **South**.

5. Change the value in cell **F6** to **180** and return to the sheet **Consol**. The profit for **Fourth Quarter** has been updated immediately.

ℹ️ *Links can also be made to cells in different workbooks as described in the* **Linking Between Workbooks** *Driving Lesson.*

6. Close the workbook <u>without</u> saving.

Driving Lesson 43 - Creating Links

▣ Park and Read

Links to cells on the same worksheet, as in a formula for example, use the simple cell reference, e.g. **=B3+B4**.

Links created between worksheets differ from cell links in that the reference includes the sheet name followed by a ! e.g. **=Sheet2!C10**.

To create a **Link** within a workbook, copy and paste from one sheet to another or start entering a formula and point to the required cell/s in other sheets.

Charts are either embedded on the data sheet or placed on a new sheet during the creation process. Charts are linked automatically to the base data.

A 3D-sum function can be used to consolidate data from several worksheets. This is like the normal **Sum** function but instead of adding up a column or along a row, it adds corresponding cells across adjacent worksheets.

⌒ Manoeuvres

1. Open the workbook **Links**. This shows sales data from 3 regions on separate sheets and a **Results** sheet on which to consolidate the data. Embedded charts have been created from the data on each of the sheets **North**, **South** and **Mid**. The sales and costs figures for the northern region have been charted on a separate sheet named **Chart**.

2. Click on the **North** worksheet. Charts are linked to the data automatically. Click on cell **D6** and type **5000** and press **<Enter>**. Note that not only the data changes to match the entry but that the chart is resized to accommodate the new data.

3. Charts created on separate sheets work in the same way. Click on the sheet **Chart**. Note that the **February Sales** are **5000** (and are more than the costs). Click on **North** and return the value in cell **D6** back to **3010** by typing or with **Undo**.

4. Check back to the **Chart** sheet and note that the **February Sales** figure has changed.

5. Select the **Results** sheet and in cell **C6**, enter the formula **=North!C6+South!C6+Mid!C6**, either by typing or by pointing. This creates links to cell **C6** in each regional sheet to produce a consolidated value.

6. Use the **Fill handle** to copy the formula into **D6** to **F6**. Note that relative addressing is still maintained across the sheets.

7. In **C7** enter **=SUM(North:Mid!C7)**. This is a **3D SUM** function, unlike the formula in **C6**.

Driving Lesson 43 - Continued

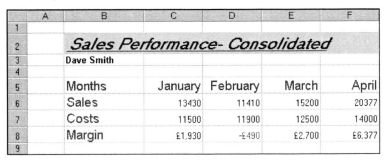

*3D-sum can also be entered using the **Autosum** button, then selecting the required cell in the **North** sheet, holding down <Shift> and clicking the **Mid** sheet tab.*

8.   Copy this formula into **D7** to **F7**.

*To enter links to single cells, **Copy** and **Paste Special** can be used.*

9.   Click cell **H2** in sheet **North** and click the **Copy** button.

10.   Click cell **B3** in sheet **Results**, select **Edit | Paste Special** and click the **Paste Link** button. This pastes a link to the Manager's name from sheet **North**, not just its current value.

	A	B	C	D	E	F
1						
2		*Sales Performance- Consolidated*				
3		Dave Smith				
4						
5		Months	January	February	March	April
6		Sales	13430	11410	15200	20377
7		Costs	11500	11900	12500	14000
8		Margin	£1,930	-£490	£2,700	£6,377
9						

11.   On sheet **North** enter your own name in **H2** as Manager. Switch to sheet **Results** and the name will have been changed.

12.   Change any **Sales** or **Cost** data on the regional sheets and the change will be reflected immediately in the charts and on the **Results** sheet.

13.   Close the workbook <u>without</u> saving.

Driving Lesson 44 - Linking Between Workbooks

Park and Read

Links created between workbooks include the source workbook name as well as the sheet and the cell reference, e.g. **=[budget.xls]Sheet1!C10**. Links are best created with the workbooks open.

If after creating a link the source workbook is closed, then the cell reference formula will also include the full location of the file, e.g.

=[C:\EXCEL\DATA\budget.xls]Sheet1!B7.

To create links between workbooks, copy from the source document and paste into the destination document using **Edit | Paste Special** and the **Paste Link** option.

Charts are simply copied from one workbook and pasted into another.

Always save the source workbook first.

Manoeuvres

1. Open the workbook **Sales**.

2. Click on the chart and copy it.

3. Start a new workbook and with the active cell as **A1**, paste the chart. The chart is linked automatically back to **Sales**.

4. In the **Sales** workbook, change the value in cell **C5** to **200000** and note the change in the new workbook.

5. Close both workbooks without saving and start a new workbook.

6. In **A1** enter **Source Document**, in cell **B3** enter a number and save the workbook as **Source**.

7. Start a new workbook. In cell **A1** enter **Container Document** and then save it as **Container**.

8. Display the two worksheets side by side with **Window | Arrange**, select the **Vertical** option and click **OK**.

9. Make **D5** active (point and click) in **Container**.

10. Create a link by typing **=**, click in the **Source** workbook to make it active and then click on cell **B3**. Press **<Enter>** to complete the formula, which should read **=[Source.xls]Sheet1!$B$3**.

Driving Lesson 44 - Continued

11. In **Source**, change the number in cell **B3**. Cell **D5** changes automatically because of the link.

12. Enter a list of 5 numbers starting in **B3** in **Source** down the column. Use the **AutoSum** button to total them in **B8**.

13. In cell **D5** in **Container**, type in the label **Total** to overwrite the earlier link.

14. Make **D6** the active cell in **Container**. Type **=** to start a formula, click in the **Source** workbook and then click on cell **B8**. Press **<Enter>** to complete the formula. The link is then created and should be;

=[Source.xls]Sheet1!$B$8.

 *An alternative method of linking is to use **Edit | Copy** at the source and then on the container sheet use **Edit | Paste Special** and the **Paste Link** button to create the link.*

15. Copy the contents in cell **B5** in **Source**. Make the workbook **Container** active, click on cell **D8** and create a link with **Edit | Paste Special** by clicking the **Paste Link** button.

16. A link has now been created between **B5** in **Source** and **D8** in **Container**. Change the number in **B5**. The numbers in cells **D6** and **D8** in **Container**, and that in **B8** in **Source** change automatically.

17. Save the workbook **Source** and close it.

18. Save the workbook **Container** and close it.

19. Open the workbook **Source**, change two of the numbers in the list and note the total.

20. Save and close the **Source** workbook.

21. Open the **Container** workbook. A message is displayed.

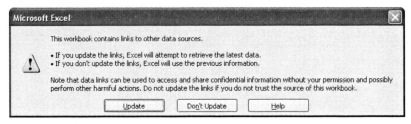

22. The links to **Source** can be updated or not as appropriate. Click **Don't Update** to leave the values unchanged.

Driving Lesson 44 - Continued

 *Clicking **Update** would have found the links in the unopened workbook and updated them, i.e. changed them to match **Source**.*

23. The links, however, can be updated at any time. To update the links, select **Edit | Links**.

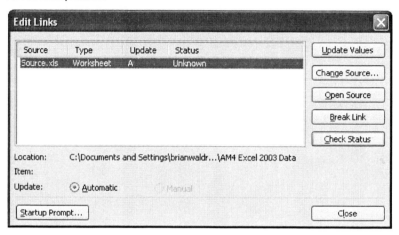

24. This dialog box controls the links in this workbook. The options are listed on the right. A link can be updated, changed or the removed. Click **Update Values**. The new total has been retrieved from the unopened workbook. Click **Close**.

25. Save the workbook **Container**.

26. To break a link, select **Edit | Links** and with the required link selected, click **Break Link**.

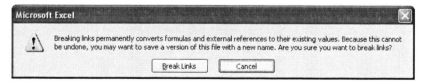

27. Read the message and then click **Break Links** to convert the cell to its existing value.

28. The link is removed. Click **Close**.

29. Close the **Container** workbook <u>without</u> saving.

Driving Lesson 45 - Linking to a Word Document

Park and Read

A spreadsheet created in *Excel* can be copied into a *Word* document. This can be done in such a way that the data is linked to the workbook it originated from and any changes to the original workbook are reflected in the *Word* document.

Manoeuvres

1. Open the workbook **Sales**. This workbook contains a spreadsheet and a chart that is to be used for linking to a word processed document.

2. Start the application *Word*.

3. In a new document, enter the text **This data is linked back to the Sales workbook**.

4. Insert two blank lines (three presses of <**Enter**>), then enter the text **Changes made in the workbook will be reflected in this document**. Press <**Enter**> twice.

5. Switch back to the **Sales** workbook in *Excel*.

6. On the **Sales** sheet, select and copy the range **B4:E7**.

7. Switch to the document in *Word*. Place the cursor between the two paragraphs.

8. Select **Edit | Paste Special**.

9. Select from the **As** box the **Microsoft Excel Worksheet Object**.

10. Select the **Paste link** option.

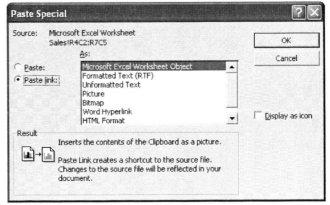

Driving Lesson 45 - Continued

11. Click **OK** to paste the range as a linked object. If the copied range is displayed as a code, select **Tools | Options**, the **View** tab and uncheck **Field Codes**. Click **OK**.

12. Switch back to *Excel*, click on the chart and copy it.

13. Switch back to *Word*.

14. Move the cursor to the end of the document, press **<Enter>** and then repeat steps **8** to **11** selecting **Microsoft Excel Chart Object** to paste the chart as a linked object in *Word*.

15. Click the **Paste Options Smart Tag** check the selected option is **Link to Excel Chart**.

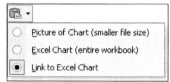

16. Note that the **May** sales for the **North** region is **£150,000**.

17. Save the *Word* document as **Linked** and close it.

18. Switch to *Excel*. Change the **May** sales figure for the **North** to **£130,000** and save the worksheet using the same name.

19. Switch back to *Word* and open the document **Linked**. In response to the message, click **Yes** to update the data from the linked workbook, **Sales**.

This data is linked back to the Sales Workbook

Company Sales	North	Central	South
May	£130,000	£110,743	£90,466
June	£140,376	£100,833	£100,744
July	£140,244	£120,500	£140,775

Changes made will be reflected in the document

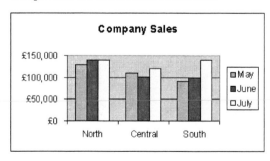

20. The cell in the table and the chart have been updated to show **£130,000**. Save the document and close the *Word* application.

21. Change the **130000** back to **150000**.

22. Save the workbook using the same name and close it.

Driving Lesson 46 - Hyperlinks

▣ Park and Read

When a spreadsheet is being viewed on screen, there are ways of making it easier for users to move to different locations within it, or to access connected information held in other locations. This is done using **hyperlinks**.

A hyperlink can be applied to a cell in a spreadsheet so that clicking the cell will display another location in the sheet which has been defined with a name. The hyperlink may also display a different worksheet, or open a different workbook. Alternatively the hyperlink can be used for reference purposes, opening a file from a different application or a web page.

⌐ Manoeuvres

1.   Open the supplied data file **Hotel**. This is a multi sheet workbook that has had names applied to some cell ranges. Make sure the **Accounts** sheet is displayed. Some hyperlinks will be added to this sheet.

2.   Click on cell **G2**, **Profit**, and click **Insert Hyperlink**, 🖳.

3.   Select **Place in This Document** from the left of the dialog box, and if necessary click the ⊞ at the left of **Defined Names** to reveal the list of available names.

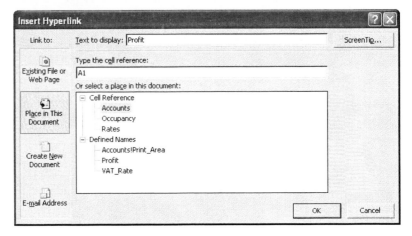

4.   Select the name **Profit**. This has been defined as applying to the **Net Profit** figures, **B34:N34** on this sheet. Click **OK**.

5.   Click on cell **H2**, **Rates**, and click **Insert Hyperlink**, 🖳.

6.   Make sure **Place in This Document** is still selected.

Driving Lesson 46 - Continued

7.   The names under **Cell Reference** represent worksheet names in this workbook. Select the worksheet name **Rates** from this list and click **OK**.

8.   Click on cell **I2**, **Information**, and click **Insert Hyperlink**, .

9.   Select **Existing File or Web Page** and **Current Folder**.

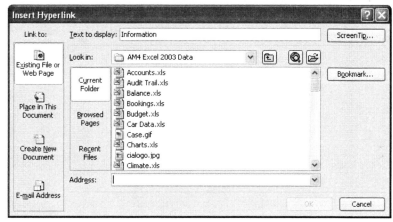

10. If necessary use the **Look in** box to locate the supplied data folder then select **Notes.doc** and click **OK**.

11. Click on cell **J2**, **Consultants**, and click **Insert Hyperlink**, . Make sure **Existing File or Web Page** is selected.

12. Type **www.ciatraining.co.uk** in the **Address** box and click **OK**.

13. On the spreadsheet move the cursor over cell **G2**, the cursor changes to a hand indicating a link. Click on cell **G2** to display the **Profit** range.

14. Click in cell **H2**. The **Rates** sheet is opened.

15. Return to the **Accounts** sheet and click cell **I2**. The **Notes** document is opened in your word processing application. This is an incorrect document the correct notes are stored in the document **Information**.

16. Close the word processing application and right click on cell **I2** the **Information** hyperlink. Select **Edit Hyperlink** and select the correct document **Information**. Click **OK**.

17. Check that the hyperlink displays the **2007** Notes. Close the word processing application and then click cell **J2**. If you have a live Internet connection the **CiA Training** web site will be opened in your browser.

18. Close your browser. To delete the hyperlink in cell **J2**, right click on it and select **Remove Hyperlink**. The hyperlink is deleted. Click on **J2** to check.

19. Leave the workbook **Hotel** open.

Driving Lesson 47 - Importing Delimited Data

P Park and Read

Data can be imported to a spreadsheet in various formats.

Data may be imported into a workbook from a text file, as long as the text file has been saved in the correct format and the text set out in such a manner that separators (tabs, commas, spaces, etc.) can be specified to split the text into the columns.

Manoeuvres

1. The workbook **Hotel** should be open. If not, open it.

2. Select **Insert | Worksheet** to add a new worksheet to the file and rename it as **Staff**.

3. Click in cell **A1** of the **Staff** worksheet then select **Data | Import External Data | Import Data**.

4. Ensure that within **Select Data Source**, the **Look in** box displays the folder containing the data. Ensure that the **Files of type** is set to **All Data Sources**. Select the file **People.txt** and click the **Open** button.

i *People.txt is a comma delimited data file which could have come from a wide range of sources. If you want to see the structure of it, open it in Notepad.*

5. The **Text Import Wizard** opens. Ensure all options are set as shown. A basic preview of the data layout is shown in the lower part of the box.

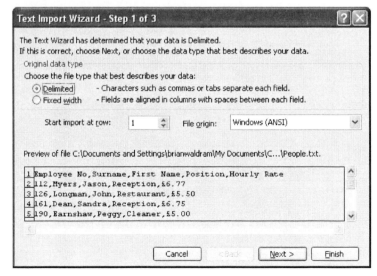

Driving Lesson 47 - Continued

6.   Click **Next** to display Step 2. Select the **Comma** option in the **Delimiters** section. Leave all other options boxes unchecked. A clearer preview of the data layout is shown in the lower part of the box.

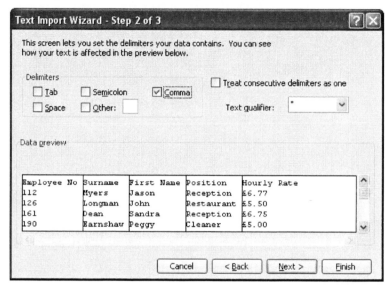

7.   Click **Next**.

8.   At Step 3 of 3 format the data in any column by selecting specific columns in the **Data preview** section and setting the required data format in the **Column data format** section. The data in all columns should be set to **General** by default. If not, correct the formats. Click **Finish**.

9.   The **Import Data** dialog box is displayed.

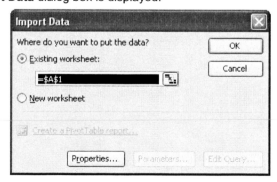

10.   Ensure that the **Existing worksheet** option is checked and the address is **A1**. Click **OK**. The data from the text file **People.txt** is imported into the empty worksheet, starting at cell **A1**.

11.   Save the workbook as **Imported** and then close it.

Driving Lesson 48 - Revision: Linking & Importing

This is not an ECDL test. Testing may only be carried out through certified ECDL test centres. This covers the features introduced in this section. Try not to refer to the preceding Driving Lessons while completing it.

1. Make sure that there are no workbooks open, even a blank workbook. Open the workbooks **Hotel2005**, **Hotel2006**, and **Hotel2007**.

2. The occupancy figures for single rooms are to be compared over the three year period. Open **Hotel Library**.

3. The single room bookings are all stored in **B7:M7** of the 3 source workbooks. The ranges to copy have all been named **singles**. Create the necessary links to **Hotel Library**.

4. With **Hotel Library** active, maximise the window. Enter the formulas to calculate % occupancy in the rows **10** to **12**, assume a **300** room per month capacity.

5. Format the range **B10:M12** as percentages to two decimal places.

6. Use **Page Setup** and **Print Preview** to set the worksheet to print on one piece of paper, landscape. Print a copy of the worksheet.

7. Save the workbook as **Hotel Occupancy**.

8. Chart the occupancy rows as a three series **Line** chart on a separate sheet (remember to include the month labels).

9. Print a copy of the chart.

10. Close all the open workbooks <u>without</u> saving.

11. What is the difference between a link and a hyperlink?

i *Check the answers at the back of the guide*

If you experienced any difficulty completing this Revision refer back to the Driving Lessons in this section. Then redo the Revision.

Once you are confident with the features, complete the Record of Achievement Matrix referring to the section at the end of the guide. Only when competent move on to the next Section.

Section 11
Sorting

By the end of this Section you should be able to:

Sort Data

Perform Multiple Column Sorts

Custom Lists and Sorts

To gain an understanding of the above features, work through the **Driving Lessons** in this **Section**.

For each **Driving Lesson**, read the **Park and Read** instructions, without touching the keyboard, then work through the numbered steps of the **Manoeuvres** on the computer. Complete the **Revision Exercise(s)** at the end of the section to test your knowledge.

Driving Lesson 49 - Sorting

▣ Park and Read

Ranges of cells in a worksheet can be sorted so that the rows in the range are arranged in a specific order. The column used to control the sort is called the **Sort Key**.

⌇ Manoeuvres

1.   Start a new workbook.

2.   Enter a column of 8 names (surnames or first names) starting in cell **B3**.

3.   Sort the names into ascending alphabetic order by placing the cursor into an occupied cell in column **B** and click the **Sort Ascending** button, ⊞.

4.   With the active cursor still in column **B** click the **Sort Descending** button, ⊞.

5.   Add ages (in years) in column **C** adjacent to the names.

6.   To sort the ages list in ascending order, place the cursor into an occupied cell in the list and select **Data | Sort**.

7.   In the first **Sort by** box select **Column C** from the drop down list and change the sort to **Ascending**. The data has **No header row**. Click **OK** to perform the sort.

8.   Close the workbook <u>without</u> saving.

Driving Lesson 50 - Multiple Column Sorts

Park and Read

In a list, the records (rows) can be sorted into a specific order based on the values of one or more of the fields (columns).

To sort a list, the method is the same as for an ordinary sort, except that the data does not have to be selected prior to sorting, selecting a cell anywhere in the list will automatically sort the whole list.

Manoeuvres

1. In a new workbook, enter the list information as shown in the rows and columns below, i.e. starting in cell **A6**.

	A	B	C	D	E	F	G
6	Make	Model	Reg.No	Engine	Colour	Mileage	Price
7	Austin	Maestro	L62 LMT	1600	Silver Grey	7124	4250
8	Vauxhall	Nova	J19 LTJ	1300	Black	74123	2250

2. Open the workbook **Car Data**.

3. To add more data to the list, copy the range **A1:G10** in **Car Data** to **A9** in the new workbook. Close the **Car Data** workbook

4. Save the workbook as **Classic Cars**.

5. Sort the list into ascending order by **Make** and perform a secondary sort by **Model**, by moving the active cell into the column under **Make** and selecting **Data | Sort**.

6. The list is defined as having a header row with **Make** in the **Sort by** box. Select **Model** in the first **Then by** box. Leave **Ascending** selected.

Driving Lesson 50 - Continued

7.   Click **OK** to perform the sort.

8.   Select **Edit | Undo Sort** to return the list to the original order.

9.   Insert a new **Column A** and set the column width to **3.00** units.

10.   Use **Edit | Fill | Series** to number each row, starting with row **7** as **1**. Label the column **No**.

11.   Sort by **Price** in descending order. Which car is the second cheapest?

12.   Sort the cars into ascending numeric order by **Mileage**. Which car has the most mileage?

13.   Using column **A** re-sort the range back to its original order.

i   *If records are to be returned to their original order after sorting, either use **Edit | Undo Sort** or better still, insert a blank column to the left and use **Edit | Fill | Series** to number each row from 1 onwards. Use **Column A** to sort back to the original order. Leading zeros may have to be added to labels that include numbers so that they sort correctly.*

14.   Save the workbook using the same file name.

15.   Close the workbook.

i   *Check the answers at the back of the guide*

Driving Lesson 51 - Custom Lists and Sorts

Park and Read

The normal **Sort** function will order items alphabetically or numerically, ascending or descending. It is however possible to sort data into any specified order using **Custom Lists**. Some **Custom Lists** are provided as defaults in *Excel*, others can be defined by the user.

Manoeuvres

1. Open the workbook **Invoices**.

2. Type **Order Day** in cell **H5**, and **Tuesday** in cell **H6.**

3. Enter a random selection of days of the week into cells **H7** to **H14** to represent the day on which each order was received. As this is a demonstration only, do not worry about matching days to the date field.

4. A normal sort on the **Order Day** column will arrange the days in alphabetical order. To sort into weekday order, click a cell in column **H** and select **Data | Sort**.

5. Make sure the **Sort by** box shows **Order Day** and click the **Options** button to display the **Sort Options** dialog box.

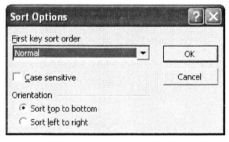

6. Use the drop down list in the **First key sort order** box to view the default custom lists available.

7. Select the list starting **Monday, Tuesday**, and click **OK** to return to the **Sort** dialog box.

Driving Lesson 51 - Continued

8.   Click **OK** to sort the list into weekday order.

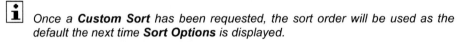

*Once a **Custom Sort** has been requested, the sort order will be used as the default the next time **Sort Options** is displayed.*

9.   Close the workbook <u>without</u> saving.

10. Open the workbook **Departments**.

11. The **Sort Options** displayed in the last diagram can be added to. This is used when a list of items is frequently used as it saves time entering them, e.g. a list of employees, departments, etc. To add a user defined **Custom List**, select **Tools | Options**. Select the **Custom Lists** tab.

12. A list can be created either by entering the items or by importing from an existing list, with **NEW LIST** selected, enter the following list, under **List entries** (use <**Enter**> between entries):

> Fred
>
> George
>
> Ann
>
> Asif
>
> Michael

13. Click **Add** then **OK**. The **Custom List** is now stored and can be used.

14. In cell **A20**, type any name from the list above. Complete the entry and use the **Fill Handle** to generate the other 4 names. Note if the list was extended is would roll round the list again.

15. A **Custom List** can also be generated from an existing list. Highlight the department list **A3:A15**. Tidy up the list by sorting it into alphabetic order.

16. With the range still highlighted, select **Tools | Options**, **Custom List** tab and click the **Import** button. Click **OK**.

17. In cell **G5** type **Sales** and generate the list down the column.

*Once **Custom Lists** have been added they can be used in any workbook.*

18. To delete the **Custom Lists** just created, select **Tools | Options**, **Custom List** tab and select each of the last two entries in turn, click **Delete**, then **OK** to confirm the deletion to remove them.

19. Click **OK** to close the **Options** dialog box.

20. Close the workbook **Departments** <u>without</u> saving.

Driving Lesson 52 - Revision: Sorting

This is not an ECDL test. Testing may only be carried out through certified ECDL test centres. This covers the features introduced in this section. Try not to refer to the preceding Driving Lessons while completing it.

1. Open the workbook **League**.

2. Sort the teams into alphabetic name order.

3. **Undo** the last operation.

4. Sort the teams into descending order of points. If the points are equal, then sort on the goal difference, again in descending order. Then sort on the number of goals-for (descending).

5. Print a copy of the **League Table**.

6. Close the workbook <u>without</u> saving.

7. Open the workbook **Supplies** which shows part of the order book for a Building Supplies Merchant.

8. Using a **Custom sort**, sort the records first by **Month Required** but in the order of **Jan**, **Feb**, etc. and then by ascending **Customer** name.

9. Print a copy of the worksheet.

10. Close the workbook <u>without</u> saving.

If you experienced any difficulty completing this Revision refer back to the Driving Lessons in this section. Then redo the Revision.

Once you are confident with the features, complete the Record of Achievement Matrix referring to the section at the end of the guide. Only when competent move on to the next Section.

Section 12
Lists

By the end of this Section you should be able to:

Filter Lists using the AutoFilter

Use Custom Criteria with AutoFilter

Use the Advanced Filter

Filter using Complex Criteria

Extract Filtered Data

Add Subtotals to a List

To gain an understanding of the above features, work through the **Driving Lessons** in this **Section**.

For each **Driving Lesson**, read the **Park and Read** instructions, without touching the keyboard, then work through the numbered steps of the **Manoeuvres** on the computer. Complete the **Revision Exercise(s)** at the end of the section to test your knowledge.

Driving Lesson 53 - Lists

▣ Park and Read

A **List** is a labelled series of rows that contain similar information - for example a list of employees, showing their names, salaries, expenses, holidays, etc. A list can be used to:

- Search or query to find specific data.

- Sort data alphabetically or numerically by rows in ascending or descending order.

- Search for matching criteria by filtering and copying to a different part of the spreadsheet.

- Perform statistical calculations on the data for analysis and decision-making.

- Print data organised for specific purposes.

A **List** separates information into columns, each containing similar information. A row contains a set of **fields**, each defined by **field names**. A completed row is a **record**. A list is composed of many such records. The field names appear as column headings with the field information below them.

	A	B	C	D	E	F	G	H	I
1	**Company Employees**								
2									
3	No	Surname	First	D.O.B.	Department	Ref No	Age	Absence	
4	1	Borland	James	30-Dec-62	Administration	AM/010	46	0	
5	2	Chapman	Ian	24-Feb-50	Finance	F/018	58	17	
6	3	Chesterton	Ian	5-May-55	Training	T/014	53	0	
7	4	Clarke	Amy	10-Apr-66	Advertising	A/007	42	0	
8	5	Collins	Paul	1-Mar-67	Administration	AM/032	41	5	
9	6	Gardner	Peter	27-Nov-74	Training	T/060	34	0	
10	7	Leigh	Clare	12-Jun-68	Administration	AM/001	40	3	
11	8	McMillan	Rose	17-Oct-59	Transport Pool	TP/040	49	1	
12	9	Myers	Anne	13-Jan-67	Computer Services	CS/085	42	0	
13	10	Parke	Neil	22-Jul-45	Training	T/040	63	1	

A sample list occupying the range A3:H13.

A field containing formulas or functions is called a computed field.

ℹ️ *Avoid having more than one list on each worksheet. Filtering can only be used on one list at a time. The **Column** labels at the top of a list can use two rows providing the labels are formatted differently to the list, e.g. font, alignment, colour, patterns etc.*

A list follows these rules:

- The area to be used must be rectangular, although it may contain blanks.

- Use the same type of data in each column.

- Do not separate the labels from the data with a blank or decorative row.

- Do not duplicate column names and to avoid confusion they should be different from any range names.

- Enter all the list information across each row.

Driving Lesson 54 - Filtering Lists

▣ Park and Read

Filtering is a quick way to find records in a list that match search criteria. Only the rows that match are displayed. The rows that do not match are hidden.

There are two ways to filter a list: the **AutoFilter** (for a simple filter) and the **Advanced Filter** (for more complex filtering). When a list is filtered, the worksheet is placed in **Filter Mode**.

	A	B	C	D	E
1					
2					
3					
4					
5					
6	Surname ▾	Initial ▾	Department ▾	Absent ▾	
7	Chapman	I	Sort Ascending	17	
8	Waldram	B	Sort Descending	2	
9	Parr	N	(All)	1	
10	Myers	A	(Top 10...)	0	
11	Westgarth	S	(Custom...)	0	
12	Smith	F	Administration / Catering	1	
13	Smith	John	Computer Services	4	
14	Gardner	P	Finance	0	
15	Leigh	C	Production / Trainee	3	
16	Collins	P	Training	5	
17	Waterman	D	Transport Pool	7	
18	McMillan	R	Transport Pool	1	
19	Wright	B	Training	4	
20	Chesterton	I	Training	0	
21	Smith	James	Production	2	
22	Borland	J	Administration	0	

*A worksheet in **Filter Mode***

In **Filter Mode**, the labels at the top of the list contain drop down arrows. If one of these arrows is clicked, a list of all items in the column is revealed. The filter to be applied can then be selected from the list.

The default view is to show all rows **(All)**, until an alternative selection is made from the list. Other options include:

> **(Top 10...)**, to show rows that fall within upper or lower limits specified by the user, e.g. top 20% of sales.

> **(Custom)**, where two criteria can be applied and data can be compared.

In the example above, all members of staff in the **Training** department can be displayed by selecting **Training** from the drop down list.

Driving Lesson 55 - AutoFilter

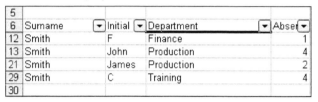 Park and Read

AutoFilter produces a subset of a list with the click of a button. This places the worksheet in **Filter Mode**. Click on any of the arrows to display a drop down list of unique items in that column. Click on any item and the matching records (rows) will be displayed with the other rows hidden.

AutoFilter always selects from the whole list. **AutoFilter** can be applied to selected columns in a list by selecting them before entering **Filter Mode**.

Manoeuvres

1. Open the workbook **Sick**.

2. Enter **Filter Mode** by clicking on a cell in the list and then selecting **Data | Filter | AutoFilter**.

3. Using the **Surname** drop down list, scroll down the list and select **Smith**. Only the Smiths are displayed.

	Surname	Initial	Department	Absen
5				
6	Surname	Initial	Department	Absen
12	Smith	F	Finance	1
13	Smith	John	Production	4
21	Smith	James	Production	2
29	Smith	C	Training	4
30				

 A filtered list can be printed.

4. To redisplay the full list using the **Surname** drop down list, select **(All)** at the top of the list.

5. Exit **Filter Mode** by selecting **Data | Filter | AutoFilter** again.

6. Open the workbook **Survey**.

7. Enter **Filter Mode**.

8. To display all the males from Sunderland who have replied, select **M** from **Sex**, **Sunderland** from **Town** and **1** from **Reply**.

 The drop down arrows are displayed in blue if active.

9. To redisplay the whole list, instead of selecting **All** from the three lists, select **Data | Filter | Show All**.

10. Exit **Filter Mode**.

11. Close the workbook **Survey** <u>without</u> saving and leave the workbook **Sick** open.

Driving Lesson 56 - Custom AutoFilter

▣ Park and Read

Custom AutoFilter allows more complicated details than a simple information match. Two conditions for selecting values within the same column can be applied by using any of the 12 options (equals, is less than, etc.). **Custom AutoFilters** can be applied both to **numbers** and **text** columns

Manoeuvres

1. The workbook **Sick** should still be open. If not, open it.

2. Using the workbook **Sick**, place the active cell inside the list and enter filter mode using **Data | Filter | AutoFilter**. Click on **Absent** and select **(Custom...)** from the drop down list to display the **Custom AutoFilter** dialog box.

*Simple searches can be carried out using one set of criteria. More complicated filters can be carried out using either **And** or **Or** then add another set of criteria.*

3. To display all the employees who have had less than five days absence, select **is less than** in the **Absent** box and enter 5 in the **Information** box.

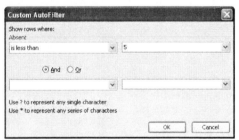

4. Click **OK**.

5. To restore the list, click on the **Absent** field drop down list and select **All**.

6. Display all the employees in either the **Administration** or **Computer Services** departments using **Custom AutoFilter** within the **Department** field, using **equals** and the **Or** option. Click **OK** to complete the filter.

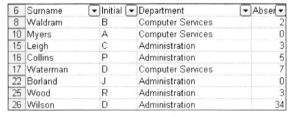

6	Surname	Initial	Department	Absen
8	Waldram	B	Computer Services	2
10	Myers	A	Computer Services	0
15	Leigh	C	Administration	3
16	Collins	P	Administration	5
17	Waterman	D	Computer Services	7
22	Borland	J	Administration	0
25	Wood	R	Administration	3
26	Wilson	D	Administration	34

7. Exit **Filter Mode** by selecting **Data | Filter | AutoFilter** again.

8. Leave the workbook **Sick** open for the next Driving Lesson.

Driving Lesson 57 - Advanced Filtering

▣ Park and Read

To search a list for more complex criteria, e.g. matching information from two fields rather than one then **Advanced Filter** is used. The **Criteria** are set up in a separate range of cells, normally to the top or right of the list. Once the **Criteria Range** has been set up, then the list can be filtered.

A **Criteria Range** can also be arranged to combine two searches by placing information on the same row (combination '**and**') or on two rows (combination '**or**'). If the same name is required for an 'and' combination the field name must be duplicated.

⌁ Manoeuvres

1. Open the workbook **Sick**, if not already open.

2. To create a criteria range, copy the field names **A6:D6** to row 1.

i *Copying the field names results in less mistakes than typing. Also copying all the names means that other filters can be performed using the same range.*

3. To setup a search for all the staff in Administration with less than 5 days absence, on row **2** enter **Administration** under **Department** and **<5** under **Absent**.

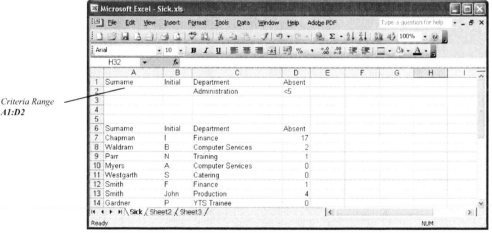

Criteria Range A1:D2

i *The criteria range must be at least one column and two rows. The first row contains the field names in any order. The other rows contain the required match information.*

4. The criteria range is now set up for the filtering to take place. Select a cell in the main list and **Data | Filter | Advanced Filter**. ☞

Driving Lesson 57 - Continued

5.　The **List range** has been defined correctly, click in the **Criteria range** box and select the range **A1:D2** (it could have been **C1:D2**, as this is all that is being used but using the larger range means that other filtering can be done with other fields without redefining the criteria range).

6.　Leave the other options as they are and click **OK** to filter the list.

	A	B	C	D
1	Surname	Initial	Department	Absent
2			Administration	<5
3				
4				
5				
6	Surname	Initial	Department	Absent
15	Leigh	C	Administration	3
22	Borland	J	Administration	0
25	Wood	R	Administration	3
30				

7.　Return to the full list in filter mode with **Data | Filter | Show All**.

8.　Try another **'and'** filter by clearing row **2** and entering new search criteria.

9.　Close the workbook <u>without</u> saving.

10.　Open the workbook **Invoices**.

11.　To filter the list using the **Invoice** and **Amount** fields, copy those two field names from row **5** to row **A1** and **B1** to set up the **Criteria Range**.

12.　To find invoice numbers less than 170 and amounts of more than £1000 excluding Vat., enter **<170** below **Invoice** and **>1000** below **Amount**.

	A	B	C
1	Invoice	Amount	
2	<170	>1000	
3			

Driving Lesson 57 - Continued

13. Select a cell in the list and **Data | Filter | Advanced Filter**.

14. Click in the **Criteria Range** box and select the range **A1:B2** on the worksheet. Click **OK** to filter the list.

5	Invoice	Date	Co. No.	Company	Amount	VAT	Total
8	167	21-Dec-06	345	J Jones	£1,345.00	£235.38	£1,580.38

15. There should only be one record. Select **Data | Filter | Show All**.

16. The last example was of an **'and'** search. To find the invoices dated before 1st Jan 2007 or totals over 750, an **'or'** search is needed. Delete the range **A1:B2** and create the following criteria range:

	A	B
1	Date	Amount
2	<1/1/07	
3		>750

17. Using **Advanced Filter** and the **Criteria Range** as **A1:B3** (to include the extra row) display the matching records (there should be **6**).

5	Invoice	Date	Co. No.	Company	Amount	VAT	Total
6	156	3-Dec-06	378	Greens	£456.00	£79.80	£535.80
7	164	15-Dec-06	294	Smith & Co	£900.00	£157.50	£1,057.50
8	167	21-Dec-06	345	J Jones	£1,345.00	£235.38	£1,580.38
9	168	21-Dec-06	387	CIA Training Ltd	£345.50	£60.46	£405.96
12	173	9-Jan-07	202	IC & JC Inc	£2,150.00	£376.25	£2,526.25
13	175	13-Jan-07	134	The Studio	£6,700.00	£1,172.50	£7,872.50

18. Click on a cell in the list and select **Data | Filter | Show All**.

19. Delete the data from the range **A1:B3**.

20. A more difficult search would involve, for example, **Amounts** between £300 and £500. This is an **and** search (on the same line) but the field name has to be given twice. Create the criteria range as below. (**AutoFilter** can do the same task and is easier).

	A	B
1	Amount	Amount
2	>300	<500

21. Use the **Advanced Filter** to display the matching records.

5	Invoice	Date	Co. No.	Company	Amount	VAT	Total
6	156	3-Dec-06	378	Greens	£456.00	£79.80	£535.80
9	168	21-Dec-06	387	CIA Training Ltd	£345.50	£60.46	£405.96
14	176	13-Jan-07	198	Car Mart	£378.00	£66.15	£444.15

22. Select to **Show All** data again.

23. Delete the data from the range **A1:B2**.

24. Leave the workbook **Invoices** open.

Driving Lesson 58 - Extracting Filtered Data

■ Park and Read

Extracting means copying records that match the criteria to another part of the worksheet. All the field names need not be used, so that specific information for a specific purpose can be extracted to form another list. The original list remains unaffected.

Manoeuvres

1. The workbook **Invoices** should still be open. If not, open it.

2. Copy the range **A5:G5** to starting cell **A1** and in cell **G2** enter **<1000** to find all the small amounts owed.

3. Select a cell in the list and then select **Data | Filter | Advanced Filter**.

4. Select **A1:G2** as the **Criteria range**.

5. Select the **Copy to another location** option.

6. Click in the **Copy to** box and then click on cell **A20**.

7. Click **OK**. The matching records are placed in a range starting **A20**.

8. Delete the range **A20:G25**.

9. Only a part of the same list is to be extracted: **Invoice**, **Company** and **Total**. Copy the three field names one at a time to the range **A20:C20**.

10. Select a cell in the list then select **Advanced Filter**, **Copy to another location** and in the **Copy to** box add the range **A20:C20**.

11. Click **OK** to extract the matching records. All the matching records are placed under the field names.

12. Close the workbook <u>without</u> saving.

Driving Lesson 59 - Adding Subtotals

Park and Read

Data in a **List** can be automatically summarised, producing subtotals based on any column. The List must first be sorted on the column for which subtotals are required. **Subtotals** are then automatically inserted on each break within that column, as well as a **Grand Total** for the whole column. Although the **SUM** function is usually used in subtotals, other functions such as **COUNT** or **AVERAGE** can be used.

When subtotals are added an **Outline View** of the list is produced grouping the data rows. This outline can be manipulated, for example to hide the detail rows and show only the subtotals.

Manoeuvres

1. Open the workbook **Sick**.

2. To display a total for the days absent, subtotalled by **Department**, first sort the list by column **C**, the **Department** column into alphabetic order.

3. Select a cell in the list and then select **Data | Subtotals...**to display the **Subtotal** dialog box.

4. Click in the **At each change in:** box and select **Department**.

5. Click in the **Use function:** box to see the possible options, but leave it set to **Sum**.

6. Make sure that in **Add subtotal to:** there is a check in the **Absent** box.

Driving Lesson 59 - Continued

7. Leave the other options as shown and click **OK**. The list is now displayed with **Absent** subtotals for each **Department**, a **Grand Total** at the end, and an **Outline view** of the list to the left of the worksheet area.

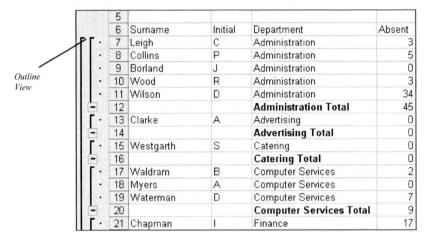

Outline View

The diagram shows only part of the Outline

8. The **Outline** view shows that there are three levels in this list, 1=Grand Total, 2=Department subtotal, 3=Detail. By default all levels are displayed on the worksheet. Click on the **Level 2** button at the top of the outline view to collapse level 3 and only show subtotals.

9. Click on the **Level 1** button to collapse subtotals and only show the grand total.

10. Individual groups may be collapsed and expanded by clicking their **Hide** buttons, ⊟, or **Show** buttons, ⊞.

11. Click the **Show** button ⊞, for the **Grand Total** to expand back to subtotals. Click the **Show** button for the **Production Total** to expand that group only.

12. Click the **Level 3** button to expand all levels again.

ℹ️ *Outline options may also be controlled from the Menu Bar.*

13. Select any cell in rows **7** to **12**.

14. Select **Data | Group and Outline | Hide Detail** to collapse the detail lines for the Administration Department.

15. Close the workbook <u>without</u> saving.

Driving Lesson 60 - Revision: Lists

This is not an ECDL test. Testing may only be carried out through certified ECDL test centres. This covers the features introduced in this section. Try not to refer to the preceding Driving Lessons while completing it.

1.   Open the workbook **Staff**.

2.   Display the **AutoFilter** and filter the list to display only the employees in the **Computer Services** department.

3.   Display all the records.

4.   Filter the list to show the employees between **40** and **50** years old inclusive.

5.   Remove the **AutoFilter**.

6.   Insert **3** more rows under row **1**.

7.   Copy the field names to row **3**.

8.   Use the **Advanced Filter** to extract a record of the employees in the **Administration** department, starting at cell **A30**.

9.   Print a copy of the workbook.

10. Close the workbook <u>without</u> saving.

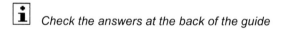 *Check the answers at the back of the guide*

If you experienced any difficulty completing this Revision refer back to the Driving Lessons in this section. Then redo the Revision.

Once you are confident with the features, complete the Record of Achievement Matrix referring to the section at the end of the guide. Only when competent move on to the next Section.

Section 13
Pivot Tables

By the end of this Section you should be able to:

Understand PivotTables

Create a PivotTable

Update a PivotTable

Filter, Group and Sort Data in a PivotTable

To gain an understanding of the above features, work through the **Driving Lessons** in this **Section**.

For each **Driving Lesson**, read the **Park and Read** instructions, without touching the keyboard, then work through the numbered steps of the **Manoeuvres** on the computer. Complete the **Revision Exercise(s)** at the end of the section to test your knowledge.

Driving Lesson 61 - PivotTables

Park and Read

A **PivotTable** organises and then summarises large amounts of data from any range that has labelled columns. Typically, two of the fields from the original data can act as the row and column headings for the new table. A third can optionally be used to group the tables into separate pages. **PivotTables** are created by default on a separate worksheet but can be created on the same sheet by entering a starting cell reference that does not overlap with the original base data.

Manoeuvres

1. Open the workbook **Survey**.

2. Click inside the list and select **Data | PivotTable and PivotChart Report**.

3. At **Step 1** of the **PivotTable and PivotChart Wizard**, leave the options as **Microsoft Excel list or database** and to create a **PivotTable**. Click **Next**.

4. At **Step 2** the **Database** is selected either by name or range, click **Next**.

5. **Step 3** provides options to place the **PivotTable** with the data, or on a separate sheet. The default option is **New worksheet**, click **Finish**. A blank **PivotTable** is placed on a new sheet with the **PivotTable Toolbar** and the **PivotTable Field List** displayed.

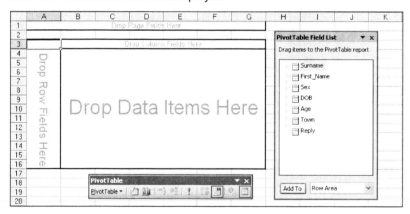

6. **Fields** are dragged from the **PivotTable Field List**, on to PivotTable areas. Drag **Town** to the **Drop Row Fields Here** section and **Sex** to the **Drop Column Fields Here** section.

Driving Lesson 61 - Continued

7. To summarise data into area by the sex of the people in the survey, drag the **Town** field on to the **Drop Data Items Here** area.

	A	B	C	D
1	Drop Page Fields Here			
2				
3	Count of Town	Sex ▼		
4	Town ▼	F	M	Grand Total
5	Bristol		2	2
6	Carlisle		1	1
7	Durham	16	17	33
8	Newcastle	17	26	43
9	South Shields	12	12	24
10	Sunderland	28	35	63
11	Tynemouth	1	2	3
12	Washington	22	29	51
13	Grand Total	96	124	220

8. The **PivotTable** is created. The data items are a count of the people surveyed, organised by town and sex.

9. Click on the sheet away from the **PivotTable** and the **PivotTable Toolbar** becomes inactive and the **PivotTable Field List** is hidden. Click inside the **PivotTable** and the **PivotTable Field List** is redisplayed.

10. To organise the table differently the fields can be changed round, i.e. pivoted. Change **Town** and **Sex** over by dragging the grey field buttons. Observe the changes then return **Town** and **Sex** to their original positions.

11. Rename the sheet **Pivot**.

12. Display the **Survey Results** sheet and make a few changes to **Town** fields (people have moved from one town to another).

13. The **PivotTable** is now out of date, click on the sheet containing the PivotTable and then click inside the table. **PivotTables** do not automatically update, click the **Refresh Data** button, ⌐✎⌐ on the **PivotTable Toolbar** to update it.

ⓘ *If the **PivotTable Toolbar** is not displayed, select **View | Toolbars** and click **PivotTable**.*

ⓘ *An alternative method to update a **PivotTable** is with the active cell inside the table select **Data | Refresh Data**.*

14. Save the workbook as **Survey2**.

15. Leave the workbook **Survey2** open for the next Driving Lesson.

Driving Lesson 62 - Filtering a PivotTable

🄿 Park and Read

Data items in a **PivotTable** can be filtered by displaying one at a time by using a drop down list. The required field is dragged to the **Page** area.

〽 Manoeuvres

1. The workbook **Survey2** should be open. If not, open it.

2. Click on the drop down arrow next to the **Town** column heading to select an area to display.

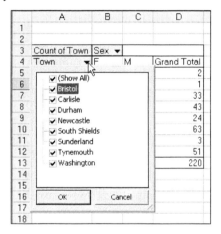

3. Remove the check from **Show All**, click the check box for **Sunderland**, and click **OK**.

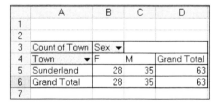

4. Specific information can also be excluded. Click the **Town** drop down arrow, check **Show All** then click the check box for **Durham** to remove its check. Click **OK**. The information for **Durham** is hidden.

5. Redisplay the information for **Durham** by clicking the **Town** drop down arrow, selecting **Durham** again and clicking **OK**.

6. Leave workbook **Survey2** open.

Driving Lesson 63 - Grouping and Sorting in PivotTables

▣ Park and Read

As well as displaying data summarised by any of the columns in the original list, **Pivot Tables** can be also be used to further arrange items into new groups. For example, with data summarised by month, January, February and March can be further grouped into Quarter1; or with data grouped by town, selected towns can be grouped to form Region 1.

Once data has been grouped, the original detail can be hidden so that only the group totals are shown.

☞ Manoeuvres

1. If the workbook **Survey2** is not open, open it now and display the sheet containing the **PivotTable**, if not already shown.

2. Sorting is performed in PivotTables in a similar way to lists. Place the cursor in the **Grand Total** column and click the **Sort Ascending** button, ⬆️. The values are sorted.

3. With the active cursor still in the **Grand Total** column, click the **Sort Descending** button, ⬇️.

4. To return the PivotTable to its original state, place the cursor in the **Town** column and click the **Sort Ascending** button, ⬆️. The towns are sorted into ascending alphabetic order.

5. The town data can be manually grouped into regions. Click to select **Durham**, hold down the **<Ctrl>** key, and click on **Sunderland** and **Washington** in Column A, then release **<Ctrl>**.

6. Select **Data | Group and Outline | Group…**to create a group containing those towns.

7. The group will be named **Group1** by default. Click on the name and change it to **Wearside**.

8. Define another group containing **Newcastle**, **South Shields** and **Tynemouth** and call it **Tyneside**.

9. Select any remaining towns and group them under the name **Other**.

Driving Lesson 63 - Continued

3	Count of Town		Sex ▾		
4	Town2 ▾	Town ▾	F	M	Grand Total
5	Other	Bristol		2	2
6		Carlisle		1	1
7	Wearside	Durham	16	17	33
8		Sunderland	28	35	63
9		Washington	22	29	51
10	Tyneside	Newcastle	17	26	43
11		South Shields	12	12	24
12		Tynemouth	1	2	3
13	Grand Total		96	124	220

The numbers shown reflect the original data, your changes will have altered these values.

 The **Group** function may also be selected by right clicking any of the selected values and selecting the **Group and Outline** option.

10. The title for the new group column has defaulted to **Town2** (being a grouping of Towns). Double click on the **Town2** title and in the **PivotTable Field** dialog box change the name to **Region**. Click **OK**

11. Click the **Region** cell and select **Data | Group and Outline | Hide Detail** to hide all individual data for towns and only show totals.

12. Click **Wearside** and select **Data | Group and Outline | Show Detail** to show the detail rows within the **Wearside** group.

13. Click **Region** and select **Data | Group and Outline | Show Detail** to show all detail rows again.

 Alternatively, double clicking a group name e.g. **Wearside,** *will toggle between* **Hide** *and* **Show** *data for that group.*

 Grouping Data *and* **Hiding/Showing** *detail is exactly the same for columns as for rows.*

14. A **PivotTable** can be amended, the row, column or count data can be changed. To change the count data to replies from the town, drag **Count of Town** out of the table area (cell **A3**) and drag **Reply** into the same **DATA** area.

3	Count of Reply		Sex ▾		
4	Region ▾	Town ▾	F	M	Grand Total
5	Other	Bristol		1	1
6		Carlisle		1	1
7	Wearside	Durham	5	6	11
8		Sunderland	11	13	24
9		Washington	10	6	16
10	Tyneside	Newcastle	4	7	11
11		South Shields	6	3	9
12		Tynemouth		2	2
13	Grand Total		36	39	75

The **PivotTable** *displays those who have replied by* **Town** *and by* **Sex.**

Driving Lesson 63 - Continued

15. PivotTables can also be automatically grouped by adding an extra field. Click on **Region** and drag it out of the PivotTable to remove it.

16. Drag the **Surname** field next to **Town** and the people are then grouped by their town. Check down the list.

	A	B	C	D	E	F
1						
2						
3	Count of Reply		Sex ▾			
4	Town ▾	Surname ▾	F	M	Grand Total	
5	Bristol	Marron		1	1	
6		West				
7	Bristol Total			1	1	
8	Carlisle	Littlethorpe		1	1	
9	Carlisle Total			1	1	
10	Durham	Ambrose				
11		Beattie				
12		Brass				
13		Brewster				
14		Carter				
15		Conroy				
16		Cooper		1	1	
17		Corner				
18		Curry				
19		Dickens				
20		Fletcher				
21		Ford				
22		Frain		1	1	
23		Hewitson	1		1	
24		Hooper		1	1	
25		Hunt				

Sample of the PivotTable Grouped by Town

17. Close the workbook <u>without</u> saving.

Driving Lesson 64 - Revision: PivotTables

This is not an ECDL test. Testing may only be carried out through certified ECDL test centres. This covers the features introduced in this section. Try not to refer to the preceding Driving Lessons while completing it.

1. Open the workbook **Staff**.

2. Create a **PivotTable** on a new sheet, making sure that the **Range** box in step 2 contains the cell range of the whole table.

3. Use **Department** as the row field and **Surname** as the data field to give a breakdown of manpower by department.

4. Insert a row into the original list (not at the end) and add your own details, assigning yourself to **Production**, ref number **P/041** and **0** absence.

5. Refresh the **PivotTable** to see the effect.

6. Print the **PivotTable**.

7. Amend the **PivotTable** by dragging the **Count of Surname** out of the table, adding **Age** as the **Column** field and **Absence** as the new data field.

8. Group the data into the following Age Groups; **Under 40, 40 - 50**, and **Over 50**. Which age group is responsible for the most absences?

9. Print a copy of the amended **PivotTable**.

10. Close the workbook <u>without</u> saving.

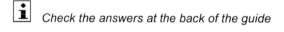 *Check the answers at the back of the guide*

If you experienced any difficulty completing this Revision refer back to the Driving Lessons in this section. Then redo the Revision.

Once you are confident with the features, complete the Record of Achievement Matrix referring to the section at the end of the guide. Only when competent move on to the next Section.

Section 14
Functions

By the end of this Section you should be able to:

Use Date and Time Functions

Use Lookup Functions

Use Mathematical and Statistical Functions

Use Financial Functions

Use Text and Database Functions

Use Nested Functions

To gain an understanding of the above features, work through the **Driving Lessons** in this **Section**.

For each **Driving Lesson**, read the **Park and Read** instructions, without touching the keyboard, then work through the numbered steps of the **Manoeuvres** on the computer. Complete the **Revision Exercise(s)** at the end of the section to test your knowledge.

Driving Lesson 65 - Functions

▣ Park and Read

Functions are specialised formulas that make calculations easier. They are grouped into categories, and some of the more common functions are listed here, grouped into the appropriate categories:

Statistical	COUNTIF, COUNTBLANK, RANK
Financial	NPV, FV, PV, PMT
Logical	IF, OR, AND, TRUE, FALSE
Math & Trig	SUMIF, ROUNDDOWN, ROUNDUP
Text	LEFT, RIGHT, MID, TRIM, CONCATENATE
Date & Time	TODAY, NOW, DAY, MONTH, YEAR
Database	DSUM, DMIN, DMAX, DCOUNT, DAVERAGE
Lookup & Reference	HLOOKUP, VLOOKUP

Statistical functions deal with analysing numerical data, from simple counting and averaging to calculating complex distribution parameters.

Financial functions deal mainly with calculations involving depreciation, loan repayments and investments over extended time scales.

Logical functions deal with the testing and setting of conditions involving **TRUE** or **FALSE** values.

Math & Trig functions deal with processing individual numerical data, from simple rounding to complex trigonometric calculations.

Text functions deal with manipulating text strings.

Date and Time functions deal with the processing and reformatting of all data relating to dates and times.

Database functions deal specifically with data, usually numeric, held in a list or database.

Lookup & Reference functions deal mainly with data in tables or ranges, for example retrieving values or transposing vertical and horizontal ranges.

Functions, like formulas, are preceded by an = sign.

Functions can be used as values in calculations.

Functions can be used within other functions (nested functions).

Driving Lesson 66 - Date and Time Functions

Park and Read

Dates and times are stored as numbers of days since 00:00 on 1st Jan 1900. Calculations using dates and times are carried out using the numbers which represent the dates and times. There are two key presses which automatically insert the current date and time.

<Ctrl ;>	Inserts the current date as text.
<Ctrl Shift ;>	Inserts the current time as text.

There are also several functions for use purely with dates and times.

DATE	Returns the number for a particular day, e.g. DATE(92,4,13) returns 33707, the number of days from 1st Jan 1900 to 13th Apr. 1992.
DAY, MONTH, YEAR	Converts a date to a number representing the day, month, or year, e.g. DAY("23/11/67") would be 23.
NOW	Used as NOW(). Returns the current date and time as a number, and is updated as the worksheet is calculated.
DATEVALUE	Converts the date as text to a number, e.g. DATEVALUE("21-Sept-49") returns 18162.
TODAY	Used as TODAY(). Returns the current date as a number and is updated as the worksheet is calculated.
WEEKDAY	Converts a number to an integer representing the day of the week from 1 (Sunday) to 7 (Saturday), e.g. WEEKDAY("21-Sept-49") returns 4, Wednesday.
TIME	Used as TIME(hour,minute,second). Returns a value in the range 0 to 0.99999999, representing a fraction of a day, e.g. TIME(16,48,10) returns 0.700115741.
TIMEVALUE	Returns a number as a fraction of the day, e.g.TIMEVALUE("22nd-Aug-67 6:35 am") returns .274305556.
HOUR, MINUTE, SECOND	Converts a time into hours, minutes, or seconds, e.g. HOUR("6:35pm") returns 18.

Driving Lesson 66 - Continued

Manoeuvres

1. Open a new workbook. This Driving Lesson shows some of the above functions in action.

2. In **B2**, enter the label **Time as number**. In **D2**, enter **Time as text**.

3. In **B4**, enter **=NOW()** and format it to display as **hh:mm:ss**. Select **Format | Cells**, **Number** tab, **Time** category and **13:30:55** format.

4. In **D4**, press **<Ctrl Shift ;>** to enter the current time.

5. In **B8**, enter the function **=TIME(8,30,0)** and custom format to display as **hh:mm**.

6. In **B12**, enter **=B4-B8** to calculate an elapsed time.

7. The **Time as number** and **Time as text** should now appear as different times. This is because the function **NOW()** is updated as the worksheet is calculated, while using **<Ctrl Shift ;>** puts text in the sheet, which is not updated.

8. In **F2**, enter **=TODAY()**. Widen the column if necessary.

9. In **F5**, enter **=DATE(** then your birthday as numbers in the form **yy,mm,dd** followed by a **)**.

10. In **F8**, enter **=F2-F5**. Format the cell as a number with no decimal places. This shows your age in days (widen the column if you are very old!!).

11. In **H5**, enter **=WEEKDAY(F5)**. This gives a number corresponding to the day of the week on which you were born (Sunday = 1, Saturday = 7).

12. In **J5** enter **=DAY(F5)** to extract the day part of your birth date.

13. In **J6** enter **=MONTH(F5)** to extract the month part of your birth date.

14. In **J7** enter **=YEAR(F5)** to extract the year part of your birth date.

15. Close the workbook <u>without</u> saving.

Driving Lesson 67 - Lookup Functions

▣ Park and Read

The **Lookup** functions are used to look up relevant data from a table, to use in a calculation. There are two functions, **HLOOKUP**, which searches a horizontal table and **VLOOKUP**, which searches a vertical table.

A **Lookup** table consists of a selection of bands, or intervals, within which a given value can be found.

⌐ Manoeuvres

1.   Open the workbook **Discount**. The worksheet consists of a discount calculation at the top and two lookup tables at the bottom, one a horizontal and one vertical, containing the same data. The discount available depends directly on the number of items bought.

2.   To use the **HLOOKUP** function, click in cell **D8**.

3.   Click the **Insert Function** button, ⨍ₓ. Select the **Lookup & Reference** category and the function name **HLOOKUP** and then click **OK**.

4.   The **Lookup_value** is cell **D4** (number bought). The **Table_array** is **C14:I15** (the table without the labels) and the **Row_index_num** is **2** (to return the value from the 2nd row of the table).

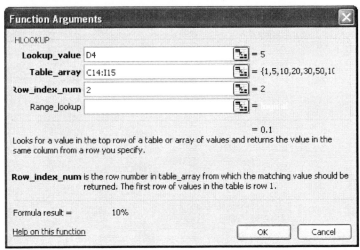

ℹ   *Setting the **Range_lookup** to **FALSE** causes the function to return a value only if there is an <u>exact</u> match between the **Lookup_value** and the table entry.*

5.   Click **OK**.

Driving Lesson 67 - Continued

6. The value returned is **10**%, corresponding to selling between 5 and 9 items.

D8			f_x =HLOOKUP(D4,C14:I15,2)	
A	B	C	D	E
1	**Lookup Tables**			
2				
3	Price		£69.95	
4	Number Bought		5	
5				
6	Total Price		£349.75	
7				
8	Discount %		10%	
9	Discount		£34.98	
10	Discount Price		£314.78	

7. Change the number bought in **D4** to **23**. The **Discount %** changes, and so does the **Discount Price**.

8. Delete the contents of cell **D8**.

9. To use the **VLOOKUP** function, click in cell **D8**.

10. Click the **Insert Function** button, ![fx]. Select the **Lookup & Reference** category and the function name **VLOOKUP** (this function is similar to **HLOOKUP** except the base data is stored in columns).

11. Click **OK**.

12. The **Lookup_value** is cell **D4** (number bought). The **Table_array** is **B19:C25** (the table without the labels) and the **Col_index_num** is **2** (to return the value from the 2nd column of the table).

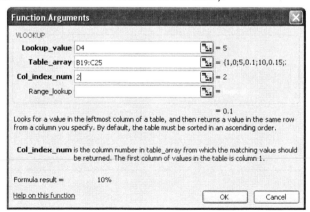

13. Click **OK** to complete the function.

14. Change the number bought in **D4** to **52**. The **Discount %** changes to **45%** the **Discount Price** is **£2000.57**.

15. Close the workbook <u>without</u> saving.

Driving Lesson 68 - Mathematical Functions

P Park and Read

SUMIF only sums values within a range that match a set condition, e.g. to sum the outstanding amounts of clients that owe more than £100.

ROUNDUP and **ROUNDDOWN** can be used to round a numeric value to any number of figures either up or down.

♞ Manoeuvres

1.　Open the workbook **Invoices**.

2.　In cell **D17**, enter the label **Small invoices total**.

3.　Select cell **E17** and click the **Insert Function** button, 📊.

i　*An alternative to the **Insert Function** button is to use the **Insert | Function** menu command.*

4.　Select the **Math & Trig** category and the function **SUMIF**. Click **OK** to display the **Function Arguments** box for **SUMIF**. Select the **Range** as **E6:E14** and enter the **Criteria** as **<500**. Click **OK**.

5.　To show the invoice totals rounded down to the nearest pound, enter **Round Down** in **H5** then select cell **H6**. Click the **Insert Function** button, 📊. Select **Math & Trig** category and the function **ROUNDDOWN**.

6.　Click **OK** to display the **Function Arguments** box for **ROUNDDOWN**.

7.　Select the **Number** as **G6**. Set the number of digits in the **Num_digits** box as **0**. Click **OK** to insert the function. The invoice total is shown rounded down to the nearest pound.

8.　Copy the function in **H6** to fill the range **H7** to **H14**.

9.　The customer would benefit from rounding down. **ROUNDUP** raises the amount higher to the specified level, usually to the next pound. Enter **Round Up** in cell **I5** then select cell **I6**.

10.　Select the **ROUNDUP** function. Select the **Number** as **G6** and set the number of digits in the **Num_digits** box as **0**. Click **OK** to insert the function. The invoice total is shown rounded up to the nearest pound

11.　Copy the function in **I6** to fill the range **I7** to **I14**.

12.　Experiment with **ROUNDUP** and **ROUNDDOWN** functions by using numbers other than 0 in the **Num_digits** box (try using 2,1,-1 and -2 to see the effects in the **Function Arguments** box).

13.　Leave the workbook open.

Driving Lesson 69 - Statistical Functions

▣ Park and Read

COUNTIF counts numeric items that match a set condition. **COUNTBLANK** counts the number of blank cells in a range. **RANK** displays a number's position in a list.

⌒ Manoeuvres

1. The workbook **Invoices** should still be open. If not, open it.

2. In cell **D16** enter the label **Invoices under £500**.

3. Select the range **E6:E14**. Select **Insert | Name | Define**.

4. **Amount** is suggested as the name for the range, click **Add** then **OK**. The range of amounts is now named **Amount** and can be used in the function.

5. Select cell **E16** and click the **Insert Function** button, .

6. Select the category **Statistical** and the function **COUNTIF**.

7. Click **OK** to display the **Function Arguments** box for **COUNTIF**.

8. In the **Range** box either type **Amount** or click and drag the range **E6:E14**. The range name is shown in the box.

9. Set the criteria in the **Criteria** box as **<500**.

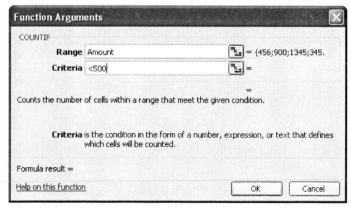

10. Click **OK**. Check the **Formula Bar** for the formula (the speech marks are added automatically). The cells that match the condition are counted.

11. Close the workbook <u>without</u> saving.

12. Open the workbook **Survey**.

Driving Lesson 69 - Continued

13. The function **COUNTBLANK** can be used to calculate the number of people who have not replied to the survey. In cell **F227** enter **Not Replied**.

14. Click in cell **G227** and click the **Insert Function** button, f_x.

15. Select the category **Statistical** and the function **COUNTBLANK**.

16. Click **OK** to display the **Function Arguments** box for **COUNTBLANK**.

17. Select the **Range** as **G6:G225**.

18. Click **OK**. The function counts the blank cells, i.e. the people who have not replied. The answer displayed is **145**.

19. The **RANK** function orders the values in a range and displays a number's position in the list, for example, the last person in the list, is he the oldest person surveyed? In cell **H225** enter **Ranked by age**.

20. Make sure that the label is left aligned.

21. Click in cell **J225** and click the **Insert Function** button, f_x.

22. Select the category **Statistical** and the function **RANK**.

23. Click **OK** to display the **Function Arguments** box for **RANK**.

24. Select **E225** as the **Number** (the last person in the list) and select the **Ref** as **E6:E225** the range of all the ages.

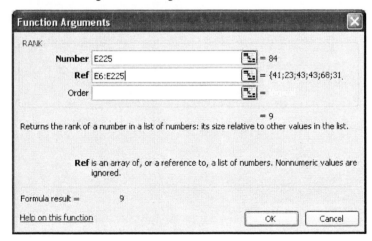

25. Click **OK**. The function ranks the selected age and displays **9**. Therefore there are eight older people surveyed in the list.

26. Close the workbook <u>without</u> saving.

Driving Lesson 70 - Text Functions

P Park and Read

The ampersand symbol, **&**, or the **CONCATENATE** function can be used to connect the contents of two or more cells that contain text. Other text manipulation functions are used to extract parts of text entries. **LEFT** extracts characters from the left, **RIGHT** extracts characters from the right, **MID** extracts characters from the middle (starting position and number of characters) and **TRIM**, used to tidy up data entry by removing space from an entry leaving only one space between words.

Manoeuvres

1. Open the workbook **Strings**.

2. On the **Strings** sheet, in **G4**, enter the formula **=A4&B4&C4**. The words are joined together, but with no spaces.

3. In **G5**, enter the function **=A4&" "&B4&" "&C4**. Each set of speech marks are around one space. This adds the spaces between the text.

4. The function **CONCATENATE** can be used to achieve the same result. In **G6**, enter the formula **=CONCATENATE(A6," ",B6," ",C6)** to achieve exactly the same effect as step 3.

5. Copy **G6** up to **G5** and **G4**.

6. The **Ref No**. is made up of the initials of the customer added to the invoice number. In **F4** enter the function **=LEFT(B4,1)&LEFT(C4,1)&D4**. This gives an individual reference number.

7. Copy the formula in **F4** down to **F5** and **F6**.

8. The stock list in cell **A11**, **0543BW00521** is made up of a part number (first 4 characters), the initials of the person who checked it (the next 2 characters) and the amount in stock (the last 5 characters).

9. In cell **B11**, enter the formula to extract the first 4 characters, the part number **=LEFT(A11,4)**. Press <**Enter**>.

10. In cell **C11**, enter the formula to extract the initials of the person who checked the item **=MID(A11,5,2)**, this starts at the 5th character and extracts 2 characters. Press <**Enter**>.

11. In cell **D11**, enter the formula to extract the last 5 characters, number of items in stock **=RIGHT(A11,5)**. Press <**Enter**>.

Driving Lesson 70 - Continued

12. In cell **A15** is an example of a driving licence. In cell **B15** use the **MID** function to extract the date of birth. The day is characters **9** and **10**. The month is characters **7** and **8**. The year is character **6** and **11**.

13. The date of birth should be **29/05/36**. Copy the formula to cell **B16**. What is this date of birth?

14. Display the **Text** sheet. This shows a small list of names where spaces have been captured in error. To tidy the display the **TRIM** function can be used.

15. In cell **C4** enter the function **=TRIM(B4)**.

16. Copy the function from **C4** down the column to cell **C12**.

17. To see the effect of **TRIM** in greater detail, the range **B4:B12** has been copied to the starting cell to **B15**. Highlight the range **B15:B23** and select **Edit | Replace**.

18. In the **Find what** box, enter a space and in the **Replace with** box enter a hash (**#**).

19. Click **Replace All**, click **OK** and then close the dialog box. This shows where the spaces were.

20. Close the workbook <u>without</u> saving.

i   *Check the answers at the back of the guide.*

Driving Lesson 71 - Financial Functions

▣ Park and Read

Three of the many financial functions deal with the repayment of loans. If **pv** is the present (original) value of the loan, **rate** is the interest rate per period, **nper** is the total number of payments and **pmt** is the repayment per period, the following functions can be used.

=PMT(rate,nper,pv)	Calculates repayments if **rate, nper** and **pv** are known.
=RATE(nper,pmt,pv)	Calculates the rate if **pmt, nper** and **pv** are known.
=PV(rate,nper,pmt,)	Calculates the loan value if **rate, pmt** and **nper** are known.

Similar functions deal with the results of investing or saving;

=FV(rate,nper,pmt)	Calculates the final value of saving an amount **pmt** for **nper** periods at **rate** percent interest.
=NPV(rate,value1,value2,..)	Calculates the net present value of an investment using a comparison discount rate of **rate** and a series of future income payments (positive values) and payments (negative values).

☞ Manoeuvres

1. Open a new workbook in which a loan repayment is to be calculated.

2. In **C2** enter the label **LOAN ANALYSIS**.

3. In **C4** enter **Interest Rate**.

4. In **C6** enter **Term (months)**.

5. In **C8** enter **Loan Amount**.

6. In **E4** enter the interest rate as **6%**.

7. The **Term** is the length of the loan. Enter **360** into **E6** (30 years).

8. In **E8** enter the size of the loan, **£50000**.

9. In **C10**, enter the label **Monthly Repayment**.

10. In **C11**, click the **Insert Function** button, . Select the **Financial** category and the payment function **PMT**. Click **OK**.

Driving Lesson 71 - Continued

11. Complete the dialog box as below:

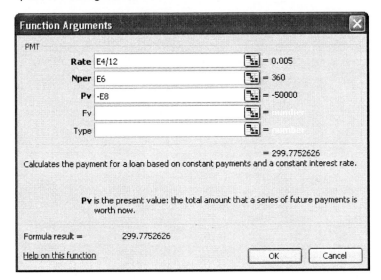

12. The **Rate** is divided by 12 to obtain a monthly rate, and the **Amount** is entered as negative because the loan is an amount owed. Click **OK** to complete the function.

13. Change the interest rate to **8%**.

14. If the maximum affordable repayment is **£300**, the maximum loan value can be calculated using **PV**.

15. In **G4** enter **8%**, in **G6** enter **360** and in **G10** enter **300**.

16. In **G8** enter the function **=PV(G4/12,G6,-G10)** to see that the maximum amount that can be borrowed.

17. To see the result of investing the same amount of money under the same conditions, in **I8** enter the function **=FV(G4/12,G6,-G10)**.

18. Save this workbook as **Loan Analysis**.

19. Close the workbook.

Check the answers at the back of the guide.

Driving Lesson 72 - Database Functions

▣ Park and Read

There are functions especially designed to be used with lists. The functions perform calculations on fields in a list, but <u>only</u> on those records which meet the selection conditions defined in the criteria range. For example in a list of sales by city, database functions can be used to obtain values for a specific city only, by selecting that city in the criteria range. The available functions are as follows.

Function	Results
DAVERAGE	Averages numbers
DCOUNT	Counts numbers
DCOUNTA	Counts nonblank cells
DGET	Extracts a single value
DMAX	Finds a maximum value
DMIN	Finds a minimum value
DPRODUCT	Multiplies numbers
DSTDEV	Calculates standard deviation of a sample
DSUM	Adds numbers
DVAR	Calculates variance of a sample

⌒ Manoeuvres

1. Open the workbook **Survey**.

2. To find information about people who have replied to the survey, copy the top line of the list, the titles, to row **2**. Rows **2** and **3** will be the area where the selection criteria for the functions will be set.

3. Enter **1** in **G3**, under **Reply**. (Only include records where **Reply** = '**1**')

4. In **I2** enter the label **Replies**, in **I4**, **Oldest**, in **I6**, **Youngest**, in **I8**, **Total** and in **I10**, **Average**.

5. Select the cell **J2** and select **Insert | Function**.

6. The **Insert Function** dialog box is displayed. Choose the category **Database** and the function **DCOUNT** from the list. Click on **OK**. The **DCOUNT** dialog box is then displayed.

Driving Lesson 72 - Continued

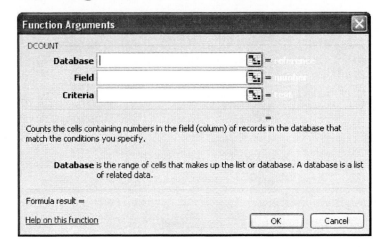

7. In **Database** enter **A5:G225**, in **field** click on **G5**.

8. In the **criteria** box, point or enter **A2:G3**.

9. Click **OK** to display the total number of replies.

10. Follow the same procedure to find the oldest person to reply. In **J4** enter = **DMAX(A5:G225,E5,A2:G3)**. Check the age field to confirm the answer.

11. In **J6** enter **=DMIN(A5:G225,E5,A2:G3)**. This displays the age of the youngest person to reply. Check the age field to confirm the answer.

12. In **J8** enter **=DSUM(A5:G225,E5,A2:G3)**. This displays the total age of all persons who have replied.

13. In **J10** enter **=DAVERAGE(A5:G225,E5,A2:G3)**. This displays the average age of all persons who have replied.

14. Close the workbook <u>without</u> saving.

 *Check the answers at the back of the guide*

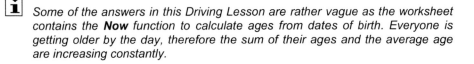 *Some of the answers in this Driving Lesson are rather vague as the worksheet contains the **Now** function to calculate ages from dates of birth. Everyone is getting older by the day, therefore the sum of their ages and the average age are increasing constantly.*

Driving Lesson 73 - Nested Functions

▣ Park and Read

Individual functions can be combined with each other to form more complex functions. When one of the values within a function is itself a function, this is known as a **Nested Function**. An example of nested text functions is **=UPPER(LEFT(B2,3))**, which would return the upper case of the left three characters in the cell **B2**.

A common use for nested functions is in the **IF** function, where the logical test, e.g. **A1>10** within **=IF(A1>10,"Yes","No")** could be replaced by another function, e.g. **AND(A1>10,A1<20)** for greater control.

It is vital that the nested function returns a value of the same type as required by the first function or an error will result. In the above examples, **LEFT** returns a text field, which is required for the **UPPER** function; **AND** returns a logical value (TRUE or FALSE) which is required as the first value for the **IF** function.

⌒ Manoeuvres

1. Open the workbook **Employees**.

2. It is decided to pay a £15 bonus to all employees 40 or over who have had less than 2 days absence this year.

3. Enter the label **Bonus** in cell **G1**

4. Select cell **G2** and click the **Insert Function** button, 🔲.

5. Select the **Logical** category and the function **IF**.

6. Click **OK** to display the **IF** box.

7. In the **Logical_test** field enter the function **AND(E2>=40,F2<2)**.

8. Enter **15** in the **Value_if_true** field and **0** in the **Value_if_false**.

9. Click **OK** to complete the function.

10. Copy the nested functions from **G2** to the range **G3** to **G20** to see who qualifies for the bonus.

11. Print a copy of the list.

12. Close the workbook <u>without</u> saving.

ℹ️ *Check the **Answers** section at the end of the guide*

Driving Lesson 74 - Revision: Functions

This is not an ECDL test. Testing may only be carried out through certified ECDL test centres. This covers the features introduced in this section. Try not to refer to the preceding Driving Lessons while completing it.

1. Open the workbook **Employees**, insert two rows at the top of the sheet and copy the column headers to the new **Row 1**.

2. In **F24** use the **COUNTIF** function to calculate the number of staff over 40 years. Manually check the age column to confirm the answer.

3. In **F25** calculate the same value using **DCOUNT**. Use **rows 1** and **2** as the **Criteria** range.

4. In **F26** use **DAVERAGE** to find the average age of staff over 40.

5. In **F27** use **ROUND** to display the average age from **F26** to the nearest whole number.

6. Without altering the functions, find the **DCOUNT** and **DAVERAGE** values for staff over 30.

7. Create the lookup table and use **HLOOKUP** to calculate an attendance bonus (**Bonus 1**) in **Column G** based on; 0-2 days absence, £50; 3-5 days, £25, 6 or more days, £0 (*when copying a HLOOKUP function down a column, remember to use absolute addressing for the lookup table*).

Absence	0	3	6
Bonus	£50	£25	£0

8. In **Column H** calculate a stress bonus (**Bonus 2**) which is **£100** for all staff in Finance or Training and **£20** for everyone else, using the **IF** function with a nested **OR** function.
    Example answer **=IF(OR(D4="Finance",D4="Training"),100,20)**.

9. Format **Column I** as numeric with 0 decimal places. In this column use the **YEAR** function to find the year of birth for each staff member and add 60 to it. Name the column **Retirement Year**.

10. In **Column J** use **CONCATENATE** to join together **First** name and **Surname** with a space between them. Widen the cells to fit the largest name and name the column **Full Name**.

11. Close the workbook <u>without</u> saving.

If you experienced any difficulty completing this Revision refer back to the Driving Lessons in this section. Then redo the Revision.

Once you are confident with the features, complete the Record of Achievement Matrix referring to the section at the end of the guide. Only when competent move on to the next Section.

Section 15
Charts

By the end of this Section you should be able to:

Add and Remove Data Series

Change Chart Types

Change Chart Axis Scales

Create Combination Charts

Add Images to Charts

To gain an understanding of the above features, work through the **Driving Lessons** in this **Section**.

For each **Driving Lesson**, read the **Park and Read** instructions, without touching the keyboard, then work through the numbered steps of the **Manoeuvres** on the computer. Complete the **Revision Exercise(s)** at the end of the section to test your knowledge.

Driving Lesson 75 - Formatting Charts

▣ Park and Read

All parts of a chart, including the colours, axes, text, gridlines, background, etc., can be changed. Two methods are available. Either double click on the required component of the chart to display the appropriate dialog box or select the component from the **Chart** toolbar and click the **Format** button .

⟨ Manoeuvres

1. Open the workbook **Charts**.

2. Click the **Sales Chart** sheet tab to display the single series column chart.

3. Move the cursor over the left axis of the chart, until the tooltip reads **Value Axis**. Double click to display the **Format Axis** dialog box.

4. Click **Scale** to display the **Scale** tab. To alter the values on the axis edit the value in the **Minimum** box to **2500**, the **Maximum** to **7500** and the **Major unit** to **500**, as below:

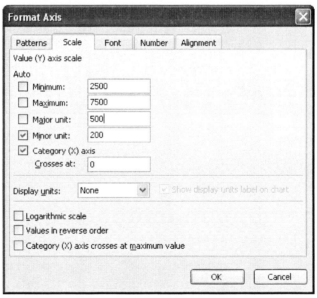

5. Click **OK** to change the axis values.

6. The values are quite large and could have been millions. The **Value Axis** can be changed to display the figures in various formats without changing the source data. Double click on the **Value Axis** again.

Driving Lesson 75 - Continued

7. The formats are changed using the **Display units** drop down box. Click the drop down arrow to the right of the box.

8. The available options are displayed. Select **Hundreds** from the list. Click **OK** to display the values in hundreds.

9. Change the display to **Thousands** using the method above (large numbers could have been displayed in millions).

10. Select **Chart | Chart Options** and display the **Data Labels** tab.

11. Various options are available to add to the series as data labels. Check the **Value** option.

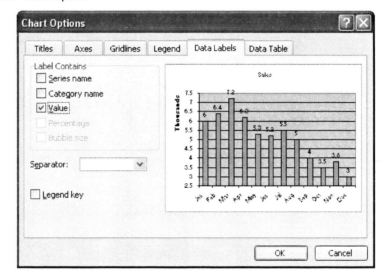

12. Click **OK** to apply. Note that the values match the axis display that was changed earlier.

13. **Data labels** are now shown and can be formatted like any other chart component. Click any **Data label** to select them all, click the **Format** button, , from the **Chart** toolbar and select the **Alignment** tab.

Driving Lesson 75 - Continued

14. The **Label Position** drop down list displays a list of available data label positions, select **Inside End**.

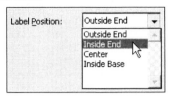

15. Click **OK**.

16. The chart title is **Sales** at the top centre. Click on the title and use the **Format** button to change the **Font** to **blue** and size **20**. Add a **light yellow** shaded background from the **Patterns** tab. Click **OK**.

17. To reposition the chart title, click on it the edge of the title and drag slightly to the left.

18. Click the **Legend** button , on the **Chart** toolbar to create a legend.

19. The **Legend** can be moved to a reset position. Select **Chart | Chart Options** and display the **Legend** tab.

20. Under **Placement** select, **Corner**, one of the five positions. Click **OK**.

21. The **Legend** can also be moved using the same technique as with moving the title. Click and drag the legend into a blank area within the chart.

22. Leave the workbook open for the next lesson.

Driving Lesson 76 - Modifying Charts

▣ Park and Read

As well as formatting the components of a chart, the chart type may be modified either globally or for individual data series. Individual data series may be removed from a chart, although this does not affect the original source data.

↱ Manoeuvres

1. The workbook **Charts** should still be open. If not open it.

2. Make the **TvS Chart** sheet active. Without selecting a particular data series, click on the drop down arrow of the **Chart Type** button, 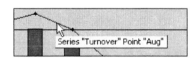, on the **Chart** toolbar.

ⓘ *The graphic on this button may vary, depending on the last used selection.*

3. From the resulting options select **Column Chart** to turn the whole chart type from 3D to 2D.

4. Click the **'Turnover'** data series (blue), making sure all columns are selected and redisplay the **Chart Type** options.

5. Select **Line Chart** (Column 1, Row 4). Now one data series is shown as columns and one as a line chart.

6. Very carefully position the cursor on the line of the **'Turnover'** data series.

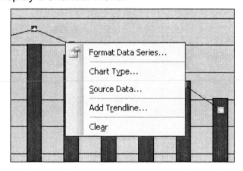

7. Right click to display a shortcut menu.

Format Data Series...
Chart Type...
Source Data...
Add Trendline...
Clear

8. Select **Clear** from the resulting menu to remove the series from the chart.

Driving Lesson 76 - Continued

9. Display the **Sales Chart**. Another **Data Series** can be added after a chart has been created.

10. To add the **Profit** figures as a series, select **Chart | Source Data**. Click on the **Series** tab. Click **Add**, collapse the **Name** box, display the **Source Data** sheet and click on the series label **A11** (the profit label).

11. Expand the **Name** box and then collapse the **Values** box, display the **Source Data** sheet and select the series **B11:M11**. Expand the **Values** box and then click **OK**. The extra data series has been added to the chart.

12. The **Legend** is on display and is expanded to include the extra series. The new series is not displayed fully as some of the values are lower than **2500**, the minimum value set previously. Change the **Minimum** to **-2500**.

13. To remove the series just added, an alternative method is to select **Chart | Source Data**, display the **Series** tab. Highlight the **Profit** series in the **Series** box and click the **Remove** button. Click **OK** to close the dialog box.

14. Change the **Minimum** back to its previously set value of **2500**.

15. Display the **TvS Chart** and change the **Chart Type** for the **Spending** data series to **Pie Chart**.

16. Click once on the chart to select all segments, each segment has a handle.

17. Drag any segment out from the centre. The whole pie chart will be exploded.

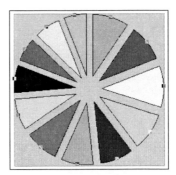

18. Push any segment back to reform the chart.

19. With the pie chart still selected, click again on a single segment to select it. This single segment can now be dragged out and pushed back.

20. Close the workbook <u>without</u> saving.

Driving Lesson 77 - Line - Column Charts

Park and Read

More than one data set can be represented on one chart to show a comparison of information. If required, each set of data on the chart can be shown in a different form, e.g. one set as columns and another set as a line. This is a **Line - Column** chart. If the two sets of data are for different types of data, e.g. temperature and rainfall, each set can have a different vertical axis. The chart is then called a **Line - Column on 2 Axes**.

Manoeuvres

1. Open the workbook **Climate**. This spreadsheet shows the rainfall and temperature for each month of the year in various cities.

2. To plot London's rainfall and temperature on a single chart, highlight the range of cells **A4:C16**, then click the **Chart Wizard** button,

3. Click the **Custom Types** tab to view other types of chart available. Scroll down and select the **Line - Column** option. Click **Next**, as the data range has already been selected, click **Next** again.

4. On the **Titles** tab, enter **London Weather** as the **Chart title**, **Date** as the **Category (X) axis**, and **Rainfall (cm)** as the **Value (Y) axis**.

5. Click **Next** and choose **As new sheet**, enter the name, **Line - Column** and click **Finish**.

6. To add a secondary axis, select **Chart | Chart Options** and display the **Axis** tab.

7. Check **Value (Y) axis** under **Secondary Axis**. Display the **Title** tab and add the text **Temperature** as the **Second value (Y) axis**. Click **OK**. A secondary axis is added to the chart.

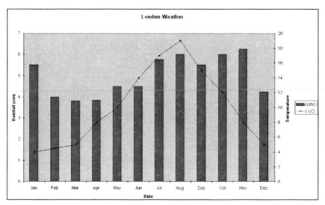

8. Save the workbook as **Climate2** and close it.

Driving Lesson 78 - Adding Images to Charts

▣ Park and Read

The use of images can greatly enhance the impact of charts. They can be used with any component of the chart but in practice they are most commonly used as backgrounds (the **Plot Area** or **Chart Area**) or as data fills for columns or bars (**Data Series**).

☞ Manoeuvres

1. Open the workbook **Charts**.

2. Make the **Sales Chart** active.

3. Click to select <u>all</u> data columns (**Series "Sales"**) and click the **Format** button on the **Chart** toolbar.

4. Select the **Options** tab and reduce the **Gap width** value to **50**. Reducing the **Gap width** increases the width of the data columns. Click **OK** to see the effect.

5. With the data columns still selected, from the **Chart** toolbar click the **Format** button, , click the **Patterns** tab and click the **Fill Effects** button.

6. Click the **Picture** tab then click the **Select Picture** button.

7. Find the image **Sales.gif** within the data files folder and double click or click and **Insert** to retrieve it.

Driving Lesson 78 - Continued

8.　Make sure that the **Stretch** option is selected, this makes the one image fill the column. Click **OK**.

9.　Click **OK** again to see the effect on the chart.

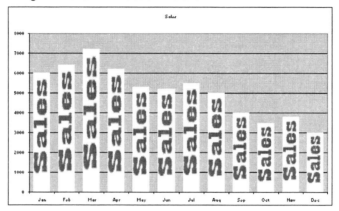

ℹ️ *Images are added to **Bar Charts** in exactly the same way.*

10.　Repeat the sequence **Format | Selected data series**, **Patterns** tab, **Fill Effects** button, **Picture** tab and **Select Picture** button.

11.　This time insert **Symbol.gif** and set the **Format** option to **Stack**.

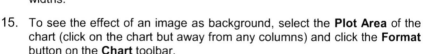

12.　Click **OK** twice to see a different style of graphic representation.

13.　Use **Format Data series** dialog box and **Patterns** tab to reset the columns to a single colour.

14.　Use **Format Data series** dialog box and **Options** to widen the gap between columns to **150**, to reduce the column widths.

15.　To see the effect of an image as background, select the **Plot Area** of the chart (click on the chart but away from any columns) and click the **Format** button on the **Chart** toolbar.

16.　In **Patterns** select **Fill Effects** button, **Picture** tab and **Select Picture** button.

17.　Insert **cialogo.jpg** and click **OK** twice to see the image fill the whole of the background (the plot area).

ℹ️ *An image is added to the **Chart Area** in exactly the same way.*

18.　Close the workbook <u>without</u> saving.

Driving Lesson 79 - Revision: Charts

This is not an ECDL test. Testing may only be carried out through certified ECDL test centres. This covers the features introduced in this section. Try not to refer to the preceding Driving Lessons while completing it.

1. Open workbook **Hotel**, and delete the blank row, **Row 3**.

2. Select the range **A3:M5** and use the **Chart Wizard** to produce a 2D column chart for the selected data series. Give the chart a title of '**Room Bookings**' and create as a new sheet.

3. Click and drag the chart title into a space in the upper left of the chart area. Click and drag the legend to position it under the title.

4. Select the **Value Axis** (vertical axis). Change the scale of the **Minimum** value to **1000**. Display **Thousands** and format the numbers with **0** decimal places.

5. Select the **Chart Area** and apply a light coloured textured background, (**Fill Effects | Texture**). Remove the colour from the **Plot Area** to increase the effect of the background.

6. Select the **Double Room** data series and change the chart type to a line chart for that series only.

7. Right click the line chart and remove it.

8. Select the remaining data series and add **Data labels**. Format the labels so that they are in the centre of the columns and align them at **90** degrees so that they appear vertical.

9. Select the data series again and add an image to it. Insert the image **Case.gif** and use the **Stack** option.

10. Set the page orientation to **Landscape** if not already set, check the print preview and then print a copy of the chart.

11. Reset the colour for the **Data Series** to **Automatic** and change the chart type to a **3D Pie** chart.

12. Select only the segment for **August** and drag it out from the rest to explode it.

13. Close down the workbook <u>without</u> saving.

If you experienced any difficulty completing this Revision refer back to the Driving Lessons in this section. Then redo the Revision.

Once you are confident with the features, complete the Record of Achievement Matrix referring to the section at the end of the guide. Only when competent move on to the next Section.

Section 16
Data Tables

By the end of this Section you should be able to:

Create a One Input Data Table

Create a Two Input Data Table

To gain an understanding of the above features, work through the **Driving Lessons** in this **Section**.

For each **Driving Lesson**, read the **Park and Read** instructions, without touching the keyboard, then work through the numbered steps of the **Manoeuvres** on the computer. Complete the **Revision Exercise(s)** at the end of the section to test your knowledge.

Driving Lesson 80 - One Input Data Table

Park and Read

A **Data Table** is used to see how changing one variable in a formula affects the result of that formula, e.g. "How do the repayments on a loan change for different interest rates?" By using a **Data Table**, the calculation need only be done once and the results of numerous different rates can be seen.

Any function can be used as the starting point for a data table.

Manoeuvres

1. Open the workbook **Loan**. This Driving Lesson creates a **Data Table** based on the calculated cell in **C11**.

2. In **B12** enter the interest rate **4%**.

3. Highlight the range **B12:B36** and select **Edit | Fill | Series** enter a **Step value** of **0.0025**. Click **OK** and this enters a list of interest rates rising in ¼ percentage points.

4. Format the range **B12:B36** as percentages to **2** decimal places.

5. Highlight the range **B11:C36** (the range of the **Data Table** includes the calculated cell) and select **Data | Table**.

6. The values to be substituted are in a column, click in the **Column input cell** box. The value actually changing is the interest rate, click on cell **E4**, the interest rate.

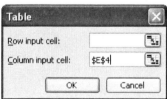

7. Click **OK**.

8. The table of values is automatically filled in, changing the repayments for different interest rates. Format the repayment figures, in column C, as currency (2 decimal places). Change the **Loan Amount** to **£60000**. The table automatically recalculates.

9. Save the workbook as **Loan2**.

10. Leave the workbook open for the next Driving Lesson.

*Part of a **Data Table** cannot be deleted. To delete a **Data Table**, the whole range must be selected.*

Driving Lesson 81 - Two Input Data Table

▣ Park and Read

A two-input data table is used to see how two variables in a formula affect the result. For instance, as well as varying the interest rate of a loan, what effect does the length of the loan have on repayments? A two input data table needs inputs for both the row and column of the table.

ℝ Manoeuvres

1. The workbook **Loan2** should still be open. If not, open it and change the **Loan Amount** back to **£50,000**.

2. Select and delete the range **C12:C36**. The range that the **Input Table** calculated.

3. Cut and paste the cell **C11** to **B11**.

4. In **C11** enter **120**. Use **Edit | Fill | Series** on the range **C11:G11**, with a step value of **60** (5 year intervals) to fill in the top row of the table.

5. Highlight the range **B11:G36** and select **Data | Table**.

6. In this table there are two inputs: a row and a column. In the **Row Input Cell**, enter E6. The **Column Input Cell** is E4. Click on **OK**. The table is instantly completed.

7. Format the table appropriately. It is now possible to see at a glance how changes in interest rates **and** loan terms alter repayments.

	A	B	C	D	E	F	G	H
1								
2			**LOAN ANALYSIS**					
3								
4			Interest Rate		8%			
5								
6			Term (months)		360			
7								
8			Loan Amount		£50,000			
9								
10			Monthly Repayment					
11		£366.88	120	180	240	300	360	
12		4.00%	£506.23	£369.84	£302.99	£263.92	£238.71	
13		4.25%	£512.19	£376.14	£309.62	£270.87	£245.97	
14		4.50%	£518.19	£382.50	£316.32	£277.92	£253.34	
15		4.75%	£524.24	£388.92	£323.11	£285.06	£260.82	
16		5.00%	£530.33	£395.40	£329.98	£292.30	£268.41	
17		5.25%	£536.46	£401.94	£336.92	£299.62	£276.10	
18		5.50%	£542.63	£408.54	£343.94	£307.04	£283.89	
19		5.75%	£548.85	£415.21	£351.04	£314.55	£291.79	
20		6.00%	£555.10	£421.93	£358.22	£322.15	£299.78	

8. Save the workbook using the same file name (**Loan2**) and close it.

ℹ️ *This example uses the **PMT** (payment) function in the **Data Table**, but any function can be used as the basis for an input data table.*

Driving Lesson 82 - Revision: Data Tables

This is not an ECDL test. Testing may only be carried out through certified ECDL test centres. This covers the features introduced in this section. Try not to refer to the preceding Driving Lessons while completing it.

1.   Open a new workbook.

2.   In **C1** enter **No. Rooms**, in **C2** enter **Charged** and in **C3** enter **Overhead**.

3.   In **E5** enter **Price Charged** and in **A12** enter **Occupied**.

4.   In **B8** enter **1** and using **Series**, produce the numbers **1** to **10** in the range **B8:B17**. This represents the number of rooms occupied.

5.   In **C7:H7** enter the numbers **15** to **20** to represent the possible charges made for each room.

6.   This table will calculate the profitability of the hotel, depending on the fixed overheads, the room charge and how many rooms are occupied. In the top left of the table, the formula for calculating the profit must be entered. In **B7** enter **=D1*D2-D3**, in **D1** enter **1**, in **D2** enter **20** and in **D3** enter **100** (the actual values in **D1** and **D2** can be left blank).

7.   Create the two-input data table.

8.   Format the data range **C8:H17** as currency, with negative numbers shown in red with a minus sign. Format the rest of the sheet appropriately.

9.   From the table, decide how many rooms the hotel must have occupied so as to guarantee a profit, regardless of the charge per room (within the charge range £15 to £20).

10. Change the overhead figure in **D3** to **130**.

11. At £20 per room the hotel is half full. Is it worth reducing the charges to £15 if this would mean it would be fully booked?

12. Obtain a printed copy.

13. Close the workbook <u>without</u> saving.

 Check the answers at the back of the guide.

If you experienced any difficulty completing this Revision refer back to the Driving Lessons in this section. Then redo the Revision.

Once you are confident with the features, complete the Record of Achievement Matrix referring to the section at the end of the guide. Only when competent move on to the next Section.

Section 17
Macros

By the end of this Section you should be able to:

Understand Macros

Record a Macro

Run a Macro

Assign a Macro to a Button on a Toolbar

To gain an understanding of the above features, work through the **Driving Lessons** in this **Section**.

For each **Driving Lesson**, read the **Park and Read** instructions, without touching the keyboard, then work through the numbered steps of the **Manoeuvres** on the computer. Complete the **Revision Exercise(s)** at the end of the section to test your knowledge.

Driving Lesson 83 - Macros

▣ Park and Read

A **Macro** is a sequence of commands which can be recorded and then played back when required. Macros are useful for automating routine tasks, simplifying complex worksheets, creating custom menus, dialog boxes and buttons and running other applications. **Macros** are usually created by recording the actual cell and menu selections themselves as they occur.

*Once recorded, **Macros** are stored as instructions written in **Visual Basic** code. It is possible to amend **Macros**, or even create them directly, by editing this code.*

*Excel has different macro security levels because of the potential threat from viruses. The default **Security** level is set to **High**. This has to be reduced for this feature to work with the accompanying data files.*

☞ Manoeuvres

1.　Select **Tools | Macro | Security** and choose from **Medium** and click **OK**.

2.　Open the workbook **Hockey**. This workbook already has macros attached to it with **Medium** security.

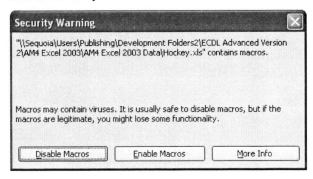

3.　Click **Enable Macros**, so that macros attached to the workbook will work.

4.　The league table has just had some results added to it. To sort the league table, select **Tools | Macro | Macros** and choose **Sort_League**.

5.　Click **Run** to carry out the sort. The league is sorted first by points, descending, then by goal difference and then by goals for.

6.　Enter **Prepared by** and your full name in cell **A12**.

7.　The command button **Print** on the worksheet has a **Print_League** macro attached. Click the **Print** button to print a copy of the league table.

8.　Close the workbook **Hockey** <u>without</u> saving.

Driving Lesson 84 - Recording a Macro

Park and Read

It is important when creating a macro that it is planned out beforehand, as *Excel* records all cell and menu selections, including mistakes!

Manoeuvres

1. Open the workbook **Hotel**. This workbook is to be used to store a variety of different macros.

2. This workbook has a **Print Area** set, select **File | Print Area | Clear Print Area** to remove it.

3. Select **Tools | Macro | Record New Macro** to display the **Record Macro** dialog box. In the **Macro name** box, enter **Name**.

4. Drop down the **Store macro in** box to see where macros can be stored.

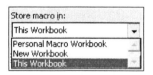

For macros to be used in any workbook they are stored in the **Personal Macro Workbook** which is opened with **Excel** although hidden. The other options are used when macros are only to be used in a single workbook.

5. Select **Personal Macro Workbook**.

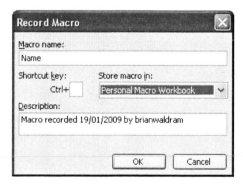

A quick key press can be used to run a macro, but care should be taken with the letter used with **Ctrl** as this will overwrite any other function the key may have already assigned to it, e.g. *<Ctrl C>* is used for copy.

6. Click **OK**.

Driving Lesson 84 - Continued

7. The word **Recording** appears on the **Status Bar** and the **Stop Recording** toolbar appears on the screen. Every key press and mouse selection is now being recorded.

Stop Recording button

8. You are to create a macro to customise your printouts by adding your name and other fields into the header/footer of all documents. Select **File | Page Setup** and display the **Header/Footer** tab.

9. Click the **Custom Footer** button. Click in the **Left section** and type your full name.

10. Click in the **Center section** and click [ ], to insert the page number field, **&[Page]**. Click in the **Right section** and click [ ] to insert the file name field, **&[File]**.

11. Click **OK** to close the **Footer** dialog box and then **OK** again to close the **Page Setup** dialog box.

ℹ️ *Information is added to the **Header** in a similar way but using the **Custom Header** button.*

12. Click the **Stop Recording** button.

ℹ️ *If you click the **Close** button of the **Stop Recording** toolbar, the recording still goes on. Select **Tools | Macro | Stop Recording** to end the recording.*

13. Create a macro for changing the page orientation to landscape. Name the macro **Landscape** and store it in the **Personal Macro Workbook**. Use **Page Setup, Page** tab to set the orientation to **Landscape**. Click **Stop Recording**.

14. A macro is to be created to apply an **AutoFormat** to a cell range. Highlight the range **A4:N34**. Create a macro, name it **Classic3** and store it in the **Personal Macro Workbook**. Select **Format | AutoFormat**, choose **Classic 3** and click **OK**. Click **Stop Recording**.

15. A macro is to be created to apply a custom number format. Click in cell **B5** and start creating a macro, name it **Format**, in the **Ctrl** box enter **f** and this time store the macro in **This Workbook**.

16. Select **Format | Cells**, display the **Number** tab and with **Currency** selected, change the **Decimal Places** to **0** and the negative numbers displayed in red with a minus sign. Click **OK** and then click **Stop Recording**.

17. Save the workbook as **Macros** and leave it open.

Driving Lesson 85 - Running a Macro

Park and Read

The macro can be activated in a variety of ways, depending on how it was set up. Some methods are covered in this Driving Lesson and the others are developed over the next few Driving Lessons. Macros can be run:

- By listing the **Macros** and selecting from the list.
- By using a key press assigned to it.
- Adding it to a **Toolbar** as a button and clicking on it.
- Assigning it to an object such as a box or a button on a sheet and clicking on it.

Manoeuvres

1. The workbook **Macros** should still be open. If not, open it.

2. Four macros have been created. The macro **Format** is the only one that can be applied to this workbook only. Highlight the range **B5:N14** and select **Tools | Macro | Macros**.

*The key press <**Alt F8**> is an alternative to the above command.*

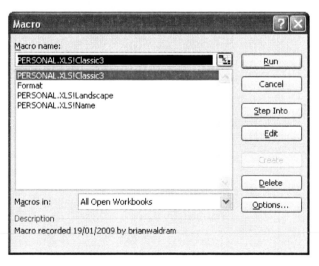

3. The **Macros** are listed. Click on the name **Format** and click **Run**. The cells are formatted with no decimal places.

4. Highlight the range **B17:N29** and use the key press <**Ctrl f**> to run the **Format** macro.

Driving Lesson 85 - Continued

Two different ways to run a macro are described in this Driving Lesson. How you choose to run a macro depends on the application and/or your personal preferences.

5. Open the workbook **League**, with the **Macros** workbook still open.

6. Print preview the **League Table** sheet. This worksheet has no header/footer and the orientation is **Portrait**. Close **Print Preview**.

7. Select **Tools | Macro | Macros**.

8. Select the **Name** macro and run it. This is checked after the next step.

9. In the same workbook run the **Landscape** macro.

10. Check the effects of the macros by previewing the worksheet, it should contain a custom footer and be in landscape orientation.

11. Close the preview.

12. Close the **League** workbook <u>without</u> saving.

13. Macros can easily be removed from a workbook. With the **Macros** workbook displayed, select **Tools | Macro | Macros**. Click on the name **Format** and click **Delete**.

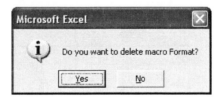

14. Click **Yes** and the macro will be deleted.

15. Close the workbook <u>without</u> saving.

Driving Lesson 86 - Assigning a Macro to a Toolbar Button

Park and Read

Macros can be added to buttons that are specifically provided and can be placed on any toolbar, in any position.

Manoeuvres

1. Open the workbook **Employees**.

2. Select **Tools | Customize**.

3. Select the **Commands** tab and **Macros** in the **Categories** box.

4. Drag the **Smiling Face** button, 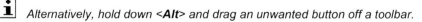, on to any displayed toolbar in any position.

5. Right click on the **Smiling Face** on the toolbar. In the **Name** box, delete what is there and type **Custom Footer** (this will be the **ToolTip**).

6. Select **Assign Macro**, choose the **Name** macro and click **OK**.

7. **Close** the **Customize** dialog box.

8. Test the macro by clicking on the **Smiling Face** button, and preview. This macro adds fields and text to the **Footer** and works with any open workbook.

9. Close the preview, start a new workbook and run the **Name** macro, by clicking.

10. Enter your first name in cell **A1** and **Print Preview** the worksheet to see the results. Close the preview.

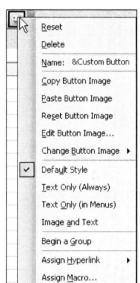

11. Close the unnamed workbook <u>without</u> saving.

12. To remove the button, select **Tools | Customize** and drag the smiling face off the toolbar.

13. Close the **Customize** dialog box.

i   *Alternatively, hold down <Alt> and drag an unwanted button off a toolbar.*

14. Close the workbook <u>without</u> saving.

Driving Lesson 87 - Revision: Macros

This is not an ECDL test. Testing may only be carried out through certified ECDL test centres. This covers the features introduced in this section. Try not to refer to the preceding Driving Lessons while completing it.

1.   Open the workbook **Macro Hotel**. This workbook contains the cash flow for a small hotel.

2.   In cell **A2** enter your name.

3.   A printout for each quarter is required. Create a macro to print the first quarter (January to March), named **Q_one**, to work only in **This workbook** and not to use a quick key press.

4.   Run the macro **Q_one** to see if it works.

5.   Create a similar macro for the second quarter (April to June), named **Q_two**.

6.   Run the macro **Q_two** to see if it works.

7.   Attach the **Landscape** macro to a custom button and place it on the **Standard Toolbar** to the right of the **Print** button, amending the **ToolTip** to **Landscape**.

8.   Preview the worksheet to check the number of pages and the orientation.

9.   Click the macro button to see if it works, check the results for landscape orientation using print preview.

10.   Remove the **Custom Button** from the **Standard Toolbar**.

11.   To delete macros stored in the workbook **Personal**, it has to be displayed. Use the **Window** drop down menu to unhide **Personal**. Delete the **Landscape** macro from the list of macros. Click **OK**.

12.   Delete the other two created macros, **Name** and **Classic3**, one at a time.

13.   Hide the **Personal** workbook now the macros have been deleted.

14.   Close the workbook **Macro Hotel** <u>without</u> saving.

15.   Close *Excel* answering **Yes** to the message about saving the changes to the **Personal Macro Workbook**.

16.   Restart *Excel* if continuing with the lessons.

If you experienced any difficulty completing this Revision refer back to the Driving Lessons in this section. Then redo the Revision.

Once you are confident with the features, complete the Record of Achievement Matrix referring to the section at the end of the guide. Only when competent move on to the next Section.

Section 18
Auditing

By the end of this Section you should be able to:

Use Auditing Tools

Trace Precedents and Dependents

Add and Remove Tracer Arrows

Trace Errors

Add Data Validation

To gain an understanding of the above features, work through the **Driving Lessons** in this **Section**.

For each **Driving Lesson**, read the **Park and Read** instructions, without touching the keyboard, then work through the numbered steps of the **Manoeuvres** on the computer. Complete the **Revision Exercise(s)** at the end of the section to test your knowledge.

Driving Lesson 88 - Auditing

🅿 Park and Read

The **Auditing** features can be used to display the structure of calculations within a spreadsheet. They can be useful in helping to track down problems, particularly in complex worksheets with many formulas. The commands are available via menus or the **Auditing Toolbar**.

📖 Manoeuvres

1. Open the workbook **Audit Trail**.

2. Select **Tools | Formula Auditing**.

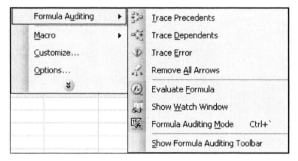

3. To display the **Auditing Toolbar** select **Show Formula Auditing Toolbar**.

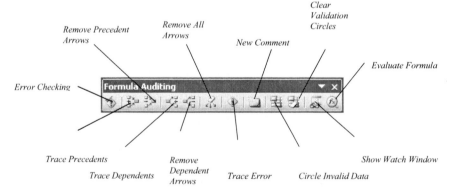

ℹ️ *If the majority of the buttons on the **Auditing** toolbar are ghosted, then select **Tools | Options**, **View** tab and check under the **Objects** section that either **Show all** or **Show placeholders** is selected. The objects must be displayed in some way for the auditing to be shown.*

4. Leave the **Auditing Toolbar** displayed and the workbook **Audit Trail** open.

Driving Lesson 89 - Tracing Precedents

P Park and Read

Precedents and **Dependents** are used to show the relationship between formulas and the cells that are used within them. **Precedents** are cells that are referenced by a formula in the current cell. Tracing **Precedents**, looks at all the cells that have been used in the current formula.

Manoeuvres

1. The workbook **Audit Trail** should still be open. If not, open it. Ensure the **Sales** sheet is active.

2. To trace precedents, click the cell **E5** and click the **Trace Precedents** button, on the **Formula Auditing** toolbar.

ⓘ *Alternatively, select **Tools | Formula Auditing | Trace Precedents**.*

	A	B	C	D	E	F
1						
2		Jan	Feb	Mar	Total	
3		13	6	4	23	
4		4	1	5	10	
5		17	7	9	33	
6						

The above diagram shows the Precedents for E5

3. With cell **E5** still selected, click the **Remove Precedent Arrows** button.

4. **Precedents** can also be traced to other worksheets or workbooks. Select the **Accounts** sheet and click on cell **C4**. Click the **Trace Precedents** button.

	A	B	C	D
	C4		*fx* =Sales!E5	
1				
2				
3				
4		Total Sales	33	
5				

*The **Precedent** is traced to another sheet/book.*

5. To check where the link is from, double click on the bullet at the end of the arrow.

6. The **Go To** dialog box is displayed showing the source of the formula. To go to the source, double click on the reference in the **Go to** box. It leads back to cell **E5** on the **Sales** sheet.

ⓘ *If the source is a different workbook it must be open, or an error is displayed.*

7. Leave the workbook **Audit Trail** open.

Driving Lesson 90 - Tracing Dependents

▣ Park and Read

Dependents are cells that reference the current cell. Tracing **Dependents** looks at all other cells where the current cell is used in a formula.

⌔ Manoeuvres

1. The workbook **Audit Trail** should still be open. If not, open it.

2. To trace **Dependents**, click on cell **C3** on the **Sales** sheet and click the **Trace Dependents** button, [⊞].

	A	B	C	D	E	F
1						
2			Jan	Feb	Mar	Total
3			13	6	4	23
4			4	1	5	10
5			17	7	9	33
6						

The above diagram shows the dependents for C3, namely cells C5 and E3

3. With cell **C3** still selected, click the **Remove Dependent Arrows** button, [⊞].

4. To trace **Dependents** to other worksheets or workbooks, select cell **E5** and click the **Trace Dependents** button, [⊞].

	A	B	C	D	E	F
1						
2			Jan	Feb	Mar	Total
3			13		4	23
4			4	1	5	10
5			17	7	9	33
6						

5. Cell **E5** is traced back to a linked worksheet/workbook. To check where the link is to, double click on the arrowhead at the end of the arrow.

6. The **Go To** dialog box is displayed showing the linked destination. Double click on the reference in the **Go to** box to go to the destination.

ⓘ *If the destination is a different workbook it must be open, or a reference error is displayed.*

7. Leave the workbook **Audit Trail** open.

Driving Lesson 91 - Tracing Errors

▣ Park and Read

Auditing tools can be used to trace an error back to the source cell/s that cause the error and identify cells with missing dependents. Tracing errors is similar to tracing precedents, but is only be used on cells that display errors.

⤴ Manoeuvres

1. The workbook **Audit Trail** should still be open. If not, open it.

2. Display the **Accounts** sheet. Cells that contain errors are displayed with a # symbol. Select cell **E11** and click the **Trace Error** button, 🔷 on the **Formula Auditing** toolbar.

9	Sales Analysis			
10		Sales Achieved	Target Sales	Performance %
11		●——33——●		🔷—●▶ #DIV/0!
12				

ℹ *Clicking this button with the active cell not containing an error, results in an error message being displayed. A **Smart Tag** is displayed, 🔷, next to the cell containing the error.*

3. Double click the arrow to highlight the cell containing the error. Cell **C11** is made active. The **Target Sales** cell has not been completed.

4. **Comments** can be attached to cells that need an explanation of the contents. Click the **New Comment** button, ▱. Enter the comment **Do not leave this cell blank**.

ℹ *Alternatively, select **Insert | Comment** to add a comment to a cell.*

5. Enter **40** in cell **C11**.

6. To remove the tracer arrows of any type, click the **Remove All Arrows** button, ▨. All the **Tracer Arrows** on the active worksheet are removed.

7. Display the **Sales** sheet. Cells containing errors can be identified by displaying the precedents of cells. Click in cell **H23** and display the **Precedents**. The correct range **B23:G23** is shown.

8. Click in Cell **H21** and trace the **Precedents**. The range is short, **B21:D21** as shown by a blue border. Amend the formula in **H21** to **B21:G21** the correct range.

9. Remove all arrows then close the **Formula Auditing Toolbar**.

10. Leave the workbook **Audit Trail** open.

Driving Lesson 92 - Data Validation

▣ Park and Read

Data Validation is used to set limits to cell entries. Existing cell content that falls outside the set limits can be highlighted using the **Circle Invalid Data** command on the **Formula Auditing** toolbar.

☞ Manoeuvres

1.   The workbook **Audit Trail** should still be open. If not, open it.

2.   Select the **Validation** sheet. This worksheet contains information about orders received from companies. To make the data entry more efficient data validation can be added to some of the ranges. All the ranges displayed with a white background contain formulas and are generated automatically.

3.   To add data validation, highlight the range **A4:A25** and select **Data | Validation** to display the **Data Validation** dialog box.

4.   The **Settings** tab is displayed. In the **Validation criteria** section, display the drop down list under **Allow**.

5.   Select each of the options in turn to view the changing **Data** areas.

6.   Select **Whole number**. If anything is selected other than the default **Any value**, then the **Data** option displays the following **Operators**:

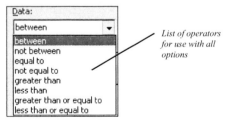

List of operators for use with all options

7.   The smallest invoice number in the range is 148. Select **greater than**. Enter **147** under **Minimum**.

Driving Lesson 92 - Continued

8. Messages can be displayed to help data entry and to point out errors. Select the **Input Message** tab. The **Title** is displayed in bold above any **Input message** when the active cell is placed on a validation cell, enter **CiA Training Ltd** in the **Title** box.

9. Enter **Invoice number** in the **Input message** box.

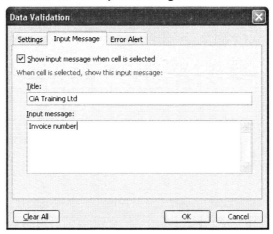

10. Select the **Error Alert** tab. This is similar to the **Input message**, except it is displayed when the validation is not met. The **Title** is displayed in the **Title Bar** of an error message dialog box. Enter **CiA Training Ltd** in the **Title** box.

11. The type of message is selected under **Style**, from **Stop**, **Warning** or **Information** (varying strengths of control). Leave the setting as **Stop**. In the **Error message** box enter **Only whole numbers over 147**.

Driving Lesson 92 - Continued

12. Click **OK** to add the validation to the range.

13. The **Input message** is displayed as the active cell is **A4**. To test the validation click on cell **A14**. Enter an invalid invoice number, i.e. a number under 148. The **Error Alert** message is displayed.

14. Click **Retry** and enter a number over **147** but add a decimal element, e.g. **180.5**. Click **Retry** and enter a valid invoice number, **181**.

15. The next column contains the invoice date, select the range **B4:B25** and add the data validation to accept **dates greater than 1/01/08**. Add suitable messages. Click **OK**.

16. Click on cell **B14**. Test the data validation by trying an invalid date first, followed by the current date.

17. The next column contains the invoice time, office hours only between **8:30** and **17:30**. Select the range **C4:C25** and add the data validation to accept office hours only (enter the times as shown above). Add suitable messages. Click **OK**.

18. Click on cell **C14**. Test the data validation by trying an invalid time first, followed by a valid time. Remember to include the colon in a time.

19. The next column is the company number which uses the company name as a lookup. The list on the right is to be used as a list to enter the company name in column **E**. Highlight the range **E4:E25**. Select **Data | Validation** and select **List** from the **Allow** drop down in the **Settings** tab. Click in the **Source** box and highlight the list of company names on the right, **K5:K13** (the names only). Click **OK**.

20. Click on cell **E14** and click the drop down to the right. This displays a list of names from which to choose.

378	Greens		£500.00
	Car Mart		
	CIA Publishing		
	Greens		
	IC & JC Inc		
	J Jones		
	Smith & Co		
	Spalding & Co		
	The Studio		

Driving Lesson 92 - Continued

21. Select a name from the list. Typing a name directly into these cells that doesn't match a name in the list results in an error message being displayed.

22. Column **F** contains the invoice amount before VAT is added. This column can contain decimals as it is for currency. Highlight the range **F4:F25**.

23. Select **Data | Validation**, then **Decimal** from the **Allow** drop down. Select the **greater than** operator and enter **0** in the **Minimum** box. Click **OK**.

24. In cell **F14** enter a negative value, then enter a valid number, **250.88**. The other two columns are completed automatically.

25. **Data Validation Circles** are a means of showing the cells that are outside the data validation restrictions placed on them. To display data validation circles, click the **Circle Invalid Data** button, ⊞, on the **Formula Auditing** toolbar.

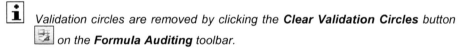

8	170	12-Mar-08	15:45	294	Smith & Co
9	172	15-Mar-08	17:35	187	White & Sons
10	173	21-Mar-08	11:38	202	IC & JC Inc

26. The only invalid entry is cell **C9** the out of office order (it was entered before the validation was added). Change **17:35** to **17:30** to make it valid.

ⓘ *Validation circles are removed by clicking the **Clear Validation Circles** button 🗗 on the **Formula Auditing** toolbar.*

27. The office hours have been extended. To edit the restrictions that are in place, highlight the range **C4:C25**, select **Data | Validation**. Change the **Start** and **End times** to **8:00** to **18:00** respectively.

ⓘ *Validation is removed using the **Clear All** button in the **Data Validation** dialog box.*

28. Click **OK** to accept the changes.

29. Leave the workbook open.

Driving Lesson 93 - Revision: Auditing

This is not an ECDL test. Testing may only be carried out through certified ECDL test centres. This covers the features introduced in this section. Try not to refer to the preceding Driving Lessons while completing it.

1. The workbook **Audit Trail** should still be open. If not, open it.

2. Select the **Validation** sheet, if not displayed and display the **Formula Auditing Toolbar**.

3. Enter a new invoice on row **15**. Invoice number **178**, invoice date **today**, in column **C** a valid time, drop the list down for the **Company** and choose **Spalding & Co** and the amount **£750**.

 The other three entries are all calculated from data entered.

4. Trace the **Precendents** of cell **H8**. What are they?

5. Trace the **Dependents** of cell **F11**. What are they?

6. Trace the **Precendents** of cell **D13**. This used the company name in **Column E** and looks up the company number from the lookup table. What are they?

7. Remove the **Precendent Arrows** from cell **D13**.

8. Add your name in cell **D1**.

9. Print a copy of the range **A1:H25**.

10. Remove all the tracer arrows.

11. Close the **Formula Auditing Toolbar**.

12. Save the workbook as **Auditing**.

13. Close the workbook.

 Check the answers at the back of the guide

If you experienced any difficulty completing this Revision refer back to the Driving Lessons in this section. Then redo the Revision.

Once you are confident with the features, complete the Record of Achievement Matrix referring to the section at the end of the guide. Only when competent move on to the next Section.

Section 19
Tracking Changes

By the end of this Section you should be able to:

Track Changes in a Worksheet

Share Workbooks

Compare and Merge Workbooks

To gain an understanding of the above features, work through the **Driving Lessons** in this **Section**.

For each **Driving Lesson**, read the **Park and Read** instructions, without touching the keyboard, then work through the numbered steps of the **Manoeuvres** on the computer. Complete the **Revision Exercise(s)** at the end of the section to test your knowledge.

Driving Lesson 94 - Track Changes in a Worksheet

▣ Park and Read

If changes to a worksheet are to be retained until further consideration has been given then **Tracking Changes** can be turned on. The changes can then be accepted or rejected at a later stage.

☞ Manoeuvres

1.   Open the workbook **Budget** and save as **Tracking**.

2.   To keep track of any changes that you make. Select **Tools | Track Changes | Highlight Changes**.

3.   Check **Track changes while editing. This also shares your workbook**.

4.   Leave **When** checked as **All**.

> **i**   *This action will also **Share your workbook**. This is used in the next Driving Lesson and is used to keep track of others changing the workbook.*

5.   Click **OK**.

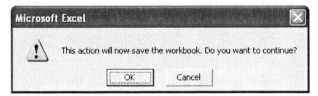

6.   Click **OK** again.

Driving Lesson 94 - Continued

7.   The workbook is now shared, check the **Title Bar**.

8.   Any changes you now make will be tracked. Change **B5** to **25**.

9.   Place the cursor over cell **B5** a comment has automatically been is attached.

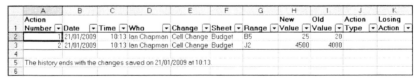

	A	B	C	D	E	F
1	Budget	Jan	Feb	Mar	Apr	May
2	Sales	6000	6400	7200	6200	5300
3	Price	6	6	6	6	6
4	Turnover	36000				800
5	Workers	⊕ 25	Ian Chapman, 21/01/2009 10:12: Changed cell B5 from '20' to '25'.			20
6	Pay	320				320
7	Wages	8000				400
8	Materials	20800				000

10. Any changes made to a **Shared** workbook are recorded. Change the **September Sales** to **4500**.

11. Save the workbook using the same file name **Tracking**.

12. The changes are saved with the workbook. These changes can be listed on a separate sheet, select **Tools | Track Changes | Highlight Changes** and check **List changes on a new sheet**. Click **OK**.

13. A **History** sheet is created with the changes listed. View the **History** sheet.

	A	B	C	D	E	F	G	H	I	J	K
1	Action Number	Date	Time	Who	Change	Sheet	Range	New Value	Old Value	Action Type	Losing Action
2	1	21/01/2009	10:13	Ian Chapman	Cell Change	Budget	B5	25	20		
3	2	21/01/2009	10:13	Ian Chapman	Cell Change	Budget	J2	4500	4000		
4											
5	The history ends with the changes saved on 21/01/2009 at 10:13.										
6											

14. The changes can be reviewed at any stage by listing each one in turn and either accepting or rejecting the change. Select **Tools | Track Changes | Accept or Reject Changes**.

Driving Lesson 94 - Continued

15. Click **OK** to continue the process.

16. **Accept** the first change and **Reject** the second. The **September Sales** reverts back to **4000**.

i *The comment is still attached to cell **B5** but has been removed from **J2**.*

17. Turning off the tracking, removes the workbook from shared use and the history of the changes is lost. Select **Tools | Track Changes | Highlight Changes**.

18. Uncheck **Track changes while editing**.

19. Click **OK**.

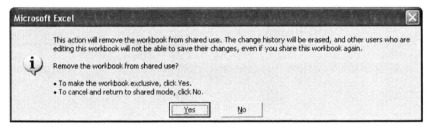

20. Click **Yes** and the workbook is automatically saved and removed from shared use.

21. Close the workbook.

Driving Lesson 95 - Shared Workbooks

Park and Read

Sharing workbooks is a way of allowing different users to update the same spreadsheet. There are two ways of doing this. The spreadsheet can be updated by different users at the same time and all the changes will be updated whenever the file is saved, or at regular intervals.

Alternatively, copies of the shared spreadsheet can be sent out to different users. Each user updates their copy then returns it. The returned copies can then be merged together, with all the changes being either accepted or ignored.

Manoeuvres

1.　Open the supplied workbook file **Hotel**. This workbook is to be shared. Save the workbook as **Communal**.

2.　To allow the workbook to be shared, select **Tools | Share Workbook**.

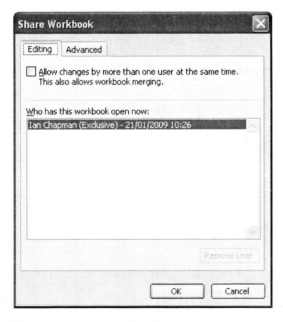

3.　Click in the **Allow changes** option box to activate it.

4.　Click the **Advanced** tab to see the settings available, then click **OK**. *Excel* will need to save the workbook with its new status and a message is displayed. Click **OK**. The workbook is saved as shared, and the **Title Bar** of the window will now show the word **Shared** next to the file name.

Driving Lesson 95 - Continued

5.   If the file is saved in an accessible location, e.g. on a server, any other user can now open and amend any part of the file (unless it is protected) while it is still open on your computer.

 *Some features cannot be applied or amended by anyone once a workbook is shared, e.g. charts, pictures, macros, hyperlinks, subtotals, scenarios, data tables, pivot tables and data validation.*

6.   If a copy of the same file was opened elsewhere, then to see who has it open, select **Tools | Share Workbook**, **Editing** tab.

7.   Click **OK**. When another user changes data in the workbook, you will be notified and see the updates when you save your copy.

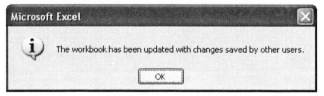

 *By changing settings in the **Advanced** view of the **Share Workbook** dialog box, the updates can be applied automatically and regularly.*

8.   Close the workbook **Communal**.

Driving Lesson 96 - Merging Workbooks

▣ Park and Read

Another way to share workbooks is to send copies out to various users so they can make their own amendments. The copies can then be merged back together, with the original user deciding which amendments to accept or ignore.

↱ Manoeuvres

1. Open the supplied workbook **Bookings** and then save it as **Holiday**. This workbook is to be sent out for review but first it must be shared.

2. Select **Tools | Share Workbook** and click in the **Allow changes** option box on the **Editing** tab.

3. Switch to the **Advanced** tab and make sure the history of changes is kept for 30 days. This means changes can be kept for up to 30 days.

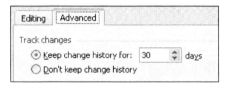

4. Click **OK** to share the workbook and **OK** again. Now the workbook can be sent out.

5. Select **File | Send To | Mail Recipient (for Review)**. Your mail application will open with a message and attachment ready to send.

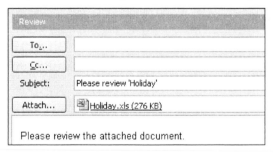

6. Address the message to another user and send it.

7. Close the workbook **Holiday**.

8. Open the workbook at its destination. If a merge changes message is displayed, click **No**. Make some small changes, e.g. change the value in cell **C5** from **2** to **4**.

Driving Lesson 96 - Continued

9. Save the amended workbook and send it back to its original user. There is a **Reply with Changes** button on the **Reviewing** toolbar which can be used for this purpose.

10. When the amended workbook is sent back, make sure it is saved in the same location as the original but with a different name, e.g. **Holiday1**. If a merge message is displayed, click **No**.

11. Open the original file **Holiday**, click **OK** to save the workbook, then select **Tools | Compare and Merge Workbooks**.

12. Select the returned file (**Holiday1**) from the **Select Files to Merge Into Current Workbook** dialog box and click **OK**.

13. To review the changes, select **Tools | Track Changes | Accept or Reject Changes**.

14. Leave the settings as shown and click **OK**. A dialog box will appear for each change in turn.

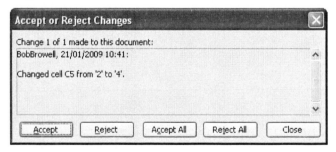

15. Each change can be accepted or rejected. If rejected, the original value will remain. Click **Accept**.

16. When there are no more dialog boxes, all changes have been reviewed. Click **End Review** on the **Reviewing** toolbar.

17. There will be up to three warning messages as you end the review process. Click **Yes** to all of them.

18. Close the workbook **Holiday**.

Driving Lesson 97 - Revision: Tracking

This is not an ECDL test. Testing may only be carried out through certified ECDL test centres. This covers the features introduced in this section. Try not to refer to the preceding Driving Lessons while completing it.

1. Open the workbook **Draft**. As the managing director of the company, you want to allow your factory manager to amend the budget predictions you have created.

2. Save the workbook as **Draft1**.

3. Set the workbook up so that it can be amended by other users while you still have it open.

 For the benefit of people without network facilities, the updates in this exercise will actually be made <u>without</u> sharing.

4. Set the workbook up to track changes while editing.

5. Save the workbook and close it.

6. Now take the part of the factory manager. Open the **Draft1** workbook.

7. You need extra workers in the summer to cover for holidays. Change the **Workers** value for **June**, **July** and **August** to **25**.

8. The canteen roof is leaking. Insert a new row above **Overheads**. Enter a label of **Repairs** and a value of **£4000** in **January**.

9. Change the **Overheads** figure for **April** to **£6000** to cover the annual golf competition. Save the workbook and close it.

10. You are now the MD again. Open the **Draft1** workbook to review your manager's changes.

11. Start the **Accept or Reject Changes** process. According to the dialog box, how many changes have been made?

12. Work through the changes, accepting the extra worker details and the overheads for the golf, but rejecting the repairs to the canteen (reject the insertion of the new row, and all associated changes will be lost).

13. You are feeling generous; add **£20** to the **Overheads** figure in **January** to buy new buckets for the canteen. What is the final **Total Net Profit** figure?

14. Remove the workbook from shared use, save it as **Draft1** and close it.

 Check the answers at the back of the guide.

If you experienced any difficulty completing this Revision refer back to the Driving Lessons in this section. Then redo the Revision.

Once you are confident with the features, complete the Record of Achievement Matrix referring to the section at the end of the guide.

Answers

Driving Lesson 3

Step 1   It is easier to manage, different people can perform different tasks, people working on one part will not have access to the rest.

Step 2   So that any scrolling will only be in one direction. This makes a spreadsheet, easier to use, easier to understand and easier to print.

Step 3   Protecting the contents of cells that do not need to be changed stops them from being deleted, even accidentally. Sensitive data can also be password protected to stop unwanted viewing.

Step 4   You may need to produce a user guide, or provide training or act as a help desk.

Step 5   **Lists** (prices, materials, customers, range of units). **Linking** (displaying prices on a calculation sheet - orders). **Formulas** and **Functions** (to perform any calculations). **Formatting** (easier to use, pleasant for customers to see, good clear printouts etc.). **Analysis** (sales figures, stock used, profit, turnover, accounts etc). **Charts** (to represent figures). Plus any other item from page 11, depending on how you approach the task.

Step 6   A **template** is a base spreadsheet with all formatting and calculations included ready for data to be added. They are used repeatedly for consistency.

Step 7   A **macro** is a tool designed to perform repetitive tasks with one action.

Step 8   As a **chart**, either: on paper, as a web page on the Internet, on a slide for a presentation.

Driving Lesson 25

Step 4   The sales figure for February is **£2,000**.

Step 5   The amount of Spending in April is **£12,720**.

Driving Lesson 34

Step 2   The IF statement entered into cell J4 should be =IF(I4=0,0,((H4-I4)/I4)). This should then be replicated down the column as far as cell J10. There are 5 cells in the workbook that contain incorrect ranges in functions:
The correct range for the function in cell H8 is (C8:G8).
The correct range for the function in cell H10 is (H4:H9).
The correct range for the function in cell E10 is (E4:E9).
The correct range for the function in cell D10 is (D4:D9).
The correct range for the function in cell K10 is (K4:K9).

Driving Lesson 48

Step 4   The formula to calculate % occupancy would be =rooms/300.

Step 8   The completed chart.

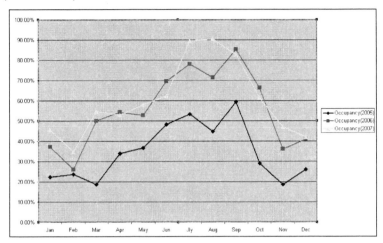

Step 11 A **link** displays data <u>from</u> another source, a **hyperlink** <u>goes</u> to another location.

Driving Lesson 50

Step 12 The second cheapest car is the **Austin Mini**.

Step 13 The car with the most mileage is the **Fiat 126**.

Driving Lesson 60

Step 2   There are 3 members of staff in the Computer Services department.

Step 4   There are 8 members of staff aged between 40 and 50 years inclusive at the time of publication of this guide.

Step 8   3 records should have been extracted.

Driving Lesson 64

Step 3   The created Pivot Table.

	A	B	C
1	Drop Page Fields Here		
2			
3	Count of Surname		
4	Department ▼	Total	
5	Administration	3	
6	Advertising	1	
7	Catering	1	
8	Computer Services	3	
9	Finance	2	
10	Personnel	2	
11	Production	2	
12	Training	4	
13	Transport Pool	1	
14	Grand Total	19	
15			

Step 8   The age group with the most absences is the **Over 50s**.

Driving Lesson 70

Step 12 =MID(A15,9,2)&"/"&MID(A15,7,2)&"/"&MID(A15,6,1)&MID(A15,11,1)

Step 13 Date of birth 28/10/57

Driving Lesson 71

Step 12 The monthly repayment is £299.78

Step 13 The repayments rise to £366.88

Step 16 The maximum amount that can be borrowed is £40,885

Step 17 The result should be £447,107

Driving Lesson 72

Step 9   There should be a total of **75** replies.

Step 10 The oldest person to reply is **96** years old.

Step 11 The youngest person to reply is **23** years old.

Step 12 The total age of all respondents should be more than **3400**.

Step 13 The average age of all respondents should be more than **46**.

Note: This workbook uses dates of birth and as a result the answers increase over time. At release these answers were correct.

Driving Lesson 73

Step 10 **8** employees qualify for the bonus.

Driving Lesson 74

Answers for this type of exercise are continually changing due to the NOW() function and therefore are not provided.

Driving Lesson 82

Step 9 7 rooms

Step 11 Yes, profit of £20 rather than loss of £30.

Driving Lesson 93

Step 4 The Precedents of cell **H8** are cells **F8** and **G8**.

Step 5 The Dependents of cell **F11** are cells **G11** and **H11**.

Step 6 The Precedents of cell **D13** are cell **E13** and the list starting at **K5**.

Driving Lesson 97

Step 11 **7** changes have been made

Step13 The total Net Profit is now **9108**

Glossary

Auditing	Allows relationships between formulas and their component cells/ranges to be displayed.
AutoFormat	Applies a set of pre-defined formatting to a worksheet in order to enhance its appearance.
AVERAGE	A function that adds the values in a range of cells, then divides the result by the number of values added.
Comment	Text that is attached to a cell as a background note. Displayed when the pointer is placed over the appropriate cell.
Concatenate	A function that can be used to combine the contents of two or more cells that contain text.
Container	A document that contains a link to a cell or range in a source document. If data in the source is modified, the container will automatically be updated.
COUNT	A function that will display the number of numerical values in a range of cells.
Data Table	Used to see how changing one variable in a formula affects its result over a range of values.
Database Function	A function that is specifically designed to be used with lists.
Dependent	A cell that is referenced in a formula.
Delimited Text	Data within a text file, where the text is separated by commas, tabs, etc. This type of data may be imported into a worksheet.
Error	A message that is displayed when a formula cannot be calculated. The nature of the message identifies the reason for the error.
Field	A cell on a row within a list.
Field Name	The heading at the top of a column of fields within a list.
Filter	A tool that matches records in a list to specified criteria.
Formula	A calculation, can use values and/or cell references.
Function	A specialised formula that makes calculations easier.
Go To	A command that can be used to navigate to a cell or range by using its reference or name.
Link	A formula reference to a cell or range in another location within the same worksheet, or another worksheet either in the same or a different workbook. A link allows data edited in the source worksheet to automatically update in the container worksheet. Links may be created to other file types.

List	A labelled series of rows that separates information into columns, each containing similar information.
Logical Function	A function that tests the contents of a cell against a specified condition to see if it is true or false. Depending on the result, the function will perform one specified action or another.
Lookup	A function that looks up relevant data from a table, and uses it in a calculation.
Macro	A recorded sequence of commands that can be replayed as required in order to automate routine tasks.
Name	Cell or range references may be replaced by names to simplify navigation around a worksheet or understanding of formulae.
Nested Function	A combination of individual functions combined with each other to perform more complex calculations.
PivotTable	A table that organises and summarises large amounts of data from within a range of labelled columns. The fields within a PivotTable may be moved (Pivoted) around between the axes and data area to analyse the data in various ways.
Precedent	A cell that is referenced by a formula.
Protection	Passwords may be used to set various levels of security for cells, worksheets or workbooks
Record	A completed row of information within a list.
Scenario	A specific combination of values and solutions that has been named and saved within a worksheet. This can then be compared to other combinations.
Source Document	A worksheet containing data that is linked to a cell or range in a container worksheet. If this data is changed, the linked cell or range will automatically be updated.
SubTotal	A function that can be applied to a list to display SUM, COUNT, or AVERAGE values of each group together with a grand total for the whole list.
SUM	A function that will add the values in a range of cells.
Summary Report	A feature that lists all existing scenarios and displays an outline view of a selected scenario.
Template	A base worksheet that provides a layout ready for data to be entered.

Index

Record of Achievement Matrix

This Matrix is to be used to measure your progress while working through the guide. This is a learning reinforcement process, you judge when you are competent.

Tick boxes are provided for each feature. 1 is for no knowledge, 2 some knowledge and 3 is for competent. A section is only complete when column 3 is completed for all parts of the section.

This is not an ECDL/ICDL test. Testing may only be carried out through certified ECDL/ICDL test centres.

Tick the Relevant Boxes **1**: No Knowledge   **2**: Some Knowledge   **3**: Competent

Section	No	Driving Lesson	1	2	3
1 Introduction	1	Spreadsheet Design		✓	
	2	Techniques to Use		✓	
2 Formatting	4	Split a Window		✓	
	5	Conditional Formatting	✓		
	6	AutoFormat		✓	
	7	Paste Special		✓	
	8	Transposing Data		✓	
	9	Copying and Moving Sheets		✓	
3 Protection	11	Protection			
	12	Worksheet and Cell Protection			
	13	Hiding Rows and Columns			
	14	Hiding Formulas			
	15	Workbook Protection			
	16	Hiding Worksheets and Workbooks			
4 Cell Comments	18	Cell Comments			
	19	Display Comments			
	20	Create, Edit & Delete Comments			
5 Names	22	Names			
	23	Using Names in Formulas			
	24	Using Go To with Names			
6 Templates	26	Creating a Template			
	27	Using a Template			
	28	Editing a Template			
7 Formulas	30	Displaying Formulas			
	31	Formulas that Produce Errors			
	32	Mixed Referencing			
	33	Custom Number Formats			

Tick the Relevant Boxes **1**: No Knowledge   **2**: Some Knowledge   **3**: Competent

Section	No	Driving Lesson	1	2	3
8 Outlines	35	Creating an Outline			
	36	Working with an Outline			
9 Scenarios	38	Creating Scenarios			
	39	Using and Editing Scenarios			
	40	Scenario Summary Reports			
10 Linking & Importing	42	Linking			
	43	Creating Links			
	44	Linking between Workbooks			
	45	Linking to a Word Document			
	46	Hyperlinks			
	47	Importing Delimited Data			
11 Sorting	49	Sorting			
	50	Multiple Column Sorts			
	51	Custom Lists and Sorts			
12 Lists	53	Lists			
	54	Filtering Lists			
	55	AutoFilter			
	56	Custom AutoFilter			
	57	Advanced Filtering			
	58	Extracting Filtered Data			
	59	Adding Subtotals			
13 Pivot Tables	61	PivotTables			
	62	Filtering a PivotTable			
	63	Grouping and Sorting in PivotTables			

Tick the Relevant Boxes **1**: No Knowledge   **2**: Some Knowledge   **3**: Competent

Section	No	Driving Lesson	1	2	3
14 Functions	65	Functions			
	66	Date and Time Functions			
	67	Lookup Functions			
	68	Mathematical Functions			
	69	Statistical Functions			
	70	Text Functions			
	71	Financial Functions			
	72	Database Functions			
	73	Nested Functions			
15 Charts	75	Formatting Charts			
	76	Modifying Charts			
	77	Line-Column Charts			
	78	Adding Images to Charts			
16 Data Tables	80	One Input Data Table			
	81	Two Input Data Table			
17 Macros	83	Macros			
	84	Recording a Macro			
	85	Running a Macro			
	86	Assigning a Macro to a Toolbar Button			
18 Auditing	88	Auditing			
	89	Tracing Precedents			
	90	Tracing Dependents			
	91	Tracing Errors			
	92	Data Validation			
19 Shared Workbooks	94	Track Changes in a Worksheet			
	95	Shared Workbooks			
	96	Merging Workbooks			

Other Products from CiA Training Ltd

CiA Training Ltd is a leading publishing company, which has consistently delivered the highest quality products since 1985. A wide range of flexible and easy to use self teach resources has been developed by CiA's experienced publishing team to aid the learning process. These include the following ECDL Foundation approved products at the time of publication of this product:

- **ECDL/ICDL Syllabus 5.0**

- **ECDL/ICDL Advanced Syllabus 2.0**

- **ECDL/ICDL Revision Series**

- **ECDL/ICDL Advanced Syllabus 2.0 Revision Series**

- **e-Citizen**

Previous syllabus versions also available - contact us for further details.

We hope you have enjoyed using our materials and would love to hear your opinions about them. If you'd like to give us some feedback, please go to:

www.ciatraining.co.uk/feedback.php

and let us know what you think.

New products are constantly being developed. For up to the minute information on our products, to view our full range, to find out more, or to be added to our mailing list, visit:

www.ciatraining.co.uk